Mathematical Thinking

in the lower secondary classroom

Edited by Christine Hopkins
Ingrid Mostert
Julia Anghileri

The Mathematical Thinking books are written by a team of lecturers and teacher trainers
from around the world who teach courses in South Africa run by the African Institute
for Mathematical Sciences Schools Enrichment Centre (AIMSSEC)

Published by Cambridge University Press,
University Printing House, Cambridge CB2 8BS, United Kingdom
Cambridge University Press is part of the University of Cambridge.

On behalf of the African Institute for Mathematical Sciences,
African Institute for Mathematical Sciences Schools Enrichment Centre,
65 Main Road, Muizenberg 7945, South Africa

It furthers the University's mission by disseminating knowledge in the pursuit of
education, learning and research at the highest international levels of excellence.

The African Institute for Mathematical Sciences Schools Enrichment Centre (AIMSSEC) is a department of The African
Institute for Mathematical Sciences, an independent educational trust (trust registration number IT3174/2002). AIMSSEC
provides professional development courses for mathematics teachers, subject advisers and field trainers to introduce new
mathematics teaching skills, to improve subject knowledge and to empower teachers. AIMSSEC works mainly with teachers
from disadvantaged rural and township communities.

First published 2016

Printed in Poland by Opolgraf

A catalogue record for this publication is available from the British Library

ISBN 978-1-316-50362-1 Paperback

Cover image: © AIMSSEC

NOTICE TO TEACHERS

....

This book is dedicated to the thousands of South African teachers who have attended AIMSSEC Mathematical Thinking courses and helped by their enthusiastic participation to develop the teaching ideas presented in this book.

Foreword for the AIMSSEC Mathematical Thinking Series

I'm delighted to be invited to write the foreword for the AIMSSEC Mathematical Thinking books. The idea originated at the very first AIMSSEC course and has been gathering momentum ever since.

The activities in these books are for any teacher of maths who wants to think more deeply about the way learners learn. All over the world, teachers teach and learners learn roughly the same maths, but in many, many different ways. These books draw on the best ideas about teaching and learning from across the world; ideas that we know, from research, have a positive impact on how learners learn.

One of the things we know from research is that teachers who are themselves learners are better equipped to help their students to be successful. We also know that doing mathematics together and talking about it helps understanding. We hope that you will be able to find a partner or group to share these activities and then use the linked classroom ideas with your own learners.

Wherever in the world you teach, mathematics is one of the most important subjects for the nation's prosperity, and for individuals' future success. It's really, really important that, as well as being fluent in basic skills, learners know what it is to behave like a mathematician, to solve problems and use their maths creatively, so that they can contribute to the future. Just as the teachers who take part in the courses have become a community committed to thinking mathematically, so too have the lecturers, teachers and researchers who together have designed and written these chapters. We hope you find them engaging and rewarding and that your learners benefit from your interest and enthusiasm, and the increased knowledge you will have acquired along the way.

Lynne McClure
Director, Cambridge Mathematics
July 2015

The AIMSSEC Mathematical Thinking series is written by a team of lecturers and teacher trainers from around the world who teach courses in South Africa run by the African Institute for Mathematical Sciences Schools Enrichment Centre (AIMSSEC), in partnership with North Western, Stellenbosch and Fort Hare Universities. The collaboration of an international writing team from Europe, USA, India, Australia, New Zealand and Africa brings a wealth of experience of classroom teaching and teacher training. The authors have experience of teaching in developing countries in every continent. Many of them are on the councils and committees of the mathematical subject associations in their own countries.

The focus is on a style of teaching based on active participation by the learners and learning through problem solving and guided re-invention. We have chosen rich activities to exemplify ways of teaching and learning that are universally relevant in the teaching of mathematics. The books provide a wealth of ideas for using easily available cost free resources in the classroom, as well as for incorporating the latest technology, particularly open source free software.

The books are designed for teachers who want to aim higher in their teaching. Each chapter provides comprehensive guidance to enable teachers to run their own workshops, and to advance their own professional development, without needing an expert leader. There are suggestions for mathematical activities to use in their teaching and for reflection and discussion about the underlying mathematical concepts together with discussion of teaching strategies appropriate to the topic.

The materials have been 'field tested' in over 500 teacher-run workshops in rural areas and townships across South Africa. These teachers come from remote rural communities and are being trained to run workshops for other teachers. The following quotations are typical of the feedback from teachers:

> "These workshops created a good relationship among the teachers at my school. It changed the mindset of those who thought that mathematics is very difficult and the activities we did made them think critically and positively."
>
> "My colleagues were amazed! These workshops changed our approach to teaching. Change is good!"
>
> "We have learnt to integrate mathematical ideas from different areas"
>
> "Instructions were simple, clear, understandable and straight forward. They were thought provoking and challenging to people's creativity."
>
> "The workshop was a real eye opener for me and for all the teachers involved."
>
> "I think as maths teachers we need more activities of this nature. Our lessons must be activity based."

The website associated with the Mathematical Thinking Series http://aiminghigh.aimssec.ac.za has interactive mathematical challenges, forums for teachers to exchange ideas and selected further readings. Both in the texts, and in the associated electronic material, we have drawn from the NRICH website http://nrich.maths.org.

Toni Beardon
AIMSSEC Founder   October 2015

Contents

Section 3: Some important teaching issues

How to use this book

This book is designed to support teachers in developing a deep understanding of the mathematics they are required to teach and in developing more effective ways of teaching.

Teachers learning together

Ideally you will be one of a group of teachers who meet together to talk about your mathematics lessons as part of your professional development. Maybe one of you will take the lead in the organising, but once you are doing the activity you will all participate in the discussion and reflection.

Each chapter has eight pages:

A **Title page** describes the curriculum content and learning outcomes. Each workshop also emphasises a particular approach to teaching or a useful technique. This is called the Teaching Strategy.

Workshop Activities for Teachers Two pages for you to work through with your colleagues. These are activities to be shared and discussed. For each activity there is a list of resources needed, how to organise the activity (e.g. pairs, whole group) and about how long the activity will take.

Classroom Activities for Learners Two pages to help you plan your lesson. You are told how long to allow for the activity, the resources you might need and the key questions to ask.

Changes in my classroom practice Three pages on implementing the teaching strategies with additional resources and activities for use during or after the workshop.

Before the workshop someone in the group will need to:

- Arrange a time and place for the teachers to meet. A workshop usually lasts around 2 hours.
- Choose a workshop that will interest the teachers in your group. You don't have to use the workshops in order.
- Photocopy the workshop. Each workshop uses a teaching strategy. The pages describing the different strategies are all at the front of the book. Photocopy the teaching strategy referred to in the title page of the workshop.
- On the title page you will find a list of the resources needed for your chosen workshop. It is essential for the success of your workshop that you have all the resources you need prepared in advance.

Enjoy the workshop. Work through the activities. When you are asked to (Try this now) please stop and try the activity before reading on. Plan when you can try the activities in your classroom. After you have done the classroom activities with your learners, it will be useful to report back to the group at your next professional development session. This would be a good time to read and discuss the Changes in my classroom practice section.

What to do if you can't get a group of teachers together

Perhaps you have a teacher friend who is happy to share some professional development with you. Most of the activities can be done by a pair. The discussion of the teaching strategy and the key questions will help you to think about how you might use the classroom activities with your learners. Again, after you have done the classroom activities with your learners, you can discuss your lessons with each other.

Further readings: This book is written for busy practising teachers so we have tried to keep the language clear and to avoid unnecessary technical terminology. We have included some references to academic papers hoping that your interest has been fired and you will want to read more about teaching strategies and mathematics learning.

Using the Classroom Activities

The activities in this book are designed to give you the skills to develop your teaching. The workshops will help your own mathematical thinking but the really important step is to develop the mathematical thinking of the learners in your classroom. Here are some possible ways of using the classroom activities.

If you will soon be teaching the workshop topic:

Make a plan for the lessons incorporating the ideas from the workshop and any other activities, workbook or textbook exercises you want to include. List the resources you will need and make plans to acquire any resources you need.

If you will soon be teaching a topic which assumes knowledge of the workshop topic:

Select activities from the workshop that can be used to review the understanding of your learners. Tackling a topic in a slightly different way will help the learners who struggled to understand the first time and be an interesting way to refresh the memory of your more confident learners.

If your learners are revising for an examination:

Learners can spend a lot of lesson time revising and this can sometimes be a dull period when the learners become concerned about all they do not know. Select some interesting activities on important topics. If you can get your learners interested and pleased with their understanding it can have a big effect on the pace at which they work and make more routine practice much more effective

Changes in my classroom practice

Whatever topic you are teaching next week you can decide to make changes and apply the teaching strategies.
- Discussion: Organise the seats and the learners so it is easy for them to discuss in pairs or in fours.
- Getting feedback: Laminate paper for showboards or use a supply of rough paper,
- People Maths: Find a large space inside or outside your school for people maths activities.
- Practical activities: Put together a basic classroom toolkit. This should include rough paper or showboards and pens, counters, string, cardboard packaging, paper clips and scissors.

Whatever topic you are teaching, use these resources to involve the learners.

Teaching Strategies

Look through the contents page and choose a topic for your workshop. As well as the mathematical content each workshop will emphasise a teaching strategy. These strategies are introduced in the following pages. They are arranged in two themes. The first is practical approaches to learning and the second is communication in the classroom.

Practical approaches to learning

Strategy 1: Visual and practical learning styles

> Visual and practical learning styles is used as a strategy in chapters: 1, 3, 7, 8, 12, 14, 15, 16, 17, 19.

Presenting a visual stimulus and really encouraging learners to look is a powerful way to focus attention in the classroom and get the learners thinking. The workshops are full of activities which use practical activities to get the learners involved and interested. Simple, inexpensive equipment such as string and counters and paper are used wherever possible. Often a short practical activity is used to develop understanding before moving to more formal tasks. **See page 4.**

Strategy 2: People maths

> People maths is used as a strategy in chapters 1, 4, 12, 14, 20.

Sometimes the resource used is the learners themselves. Learners can make a bar chart, demonstrate reflection in a mirror or demonstrate subtraction of a negative number. **See page 5.**

> **Note**
> You could return to these pages after you have tried several workshops to discuss which strategies you have found most useful in your classroom.

Strategy 1: Visual and practical learning styles

How do you remember a cell phone number? Do you 'see' it in your mind's eye?

Do you recall it by saying it?

Do you need the cell phone in front of you to tap it out?

Many people have a preference for a learning style – visual, auditory, or kinaesthetic. What this means is that, given a choice, they prefer to learn new information through seeing or hearing or doing. Of course that doesn't mean that they can't use their other senses – unless they have some specific disability they will be using all three (and others) all the time. They just learn better in one way, that's all.

So what are the implications of this for educators?

Firstly, be aware of whether you have a learning style preference and if so, what it is. (Trying the cell phone test can give you an idea, or go to the website below). The reason it is good to know is that educators tend to teach in the way that they themselves prefer to be taught. So if you prefer learning through listening you're likely to lecture your learners, if you prefer learning by using pictures and diagrams you're likely to demonstrate through illustration, and if you prefer learning by doing you're likely to set up activities where your learners have 'hands-on' experiences. Actually, of course, you should strive for a balance of instructional methods so that all your learners meet a variety of experiences. So whatever you are teaching, try to make sure that you:

- Provide some visual clues and use diagrams and pictures. Ask learners to draw their own representations of the maths you are doing together. Ask them to close their eyes and answer questions about a mathematical object they can visualise, such as a 3 dimensional shape, or the number line, or a graph...

- Give a good verbal explanation, expect learners to talk about what they are doing, and ask them to explain their ideas to you and to each other... (you can't do maths if you don't talk maths).

- Make sure that your learners have to DO something – with resources, or perhaps by moving their own bodies. There are lots of everyday objects that can be used to model mathematics... buttons, bottle tops, stones, string, straws....

Everyday objects used for sequences

Try thinking about a recent lesson you have taught and see what learning styles you and your learners used. You might be surprised!

Further reading

Richard Felder 2007 www4.ncsu.edu/unity/lockers/users/f/felder/public/Learning_Styles.html

Strategy 2: People maths

Have you ever: sung in a choir, played sport in a team, played in a band, acted in a play?

Such activities are often very memorable; we get pleasure from being involved, from being active. Young people are full of energy and we need to harness that energy to assist their learning. Throughout this book you will find activities that get the learners out of their seats and taking part in a mathematical activity. These are called People Maths activities.

Some examples of people maths activities are:

- Making string patterns based on factors (see page 17 in chapter 1)
- Using showboards for an activity on subtracting negative numbers (see page 41 in chapter 4)
- Working with brackets (see page 96 in chapter 11)
- Turning through an angle and angles in a polygon (see pages 104 and 105 and in chapter 12)
- Acting out reflection in a mirror (see page 121 in chapter 14)
- Forming a grouped bar graph or a pie chart (see pages 168 and 169 in chapter 20)

Once you have tried a few of these activities and found the ones which are most effective in involving your learners you will find that you can use people maths when you are teaching lots of different topics. The activities are designed to help the learners understand the maths. When you have moved to form a reflection in a mirror you do not forget that the image is the same distance from the mirror as the object. Wherever you use counters or draw diagrams you could instead use people and perhaps a few props like string to bring the maths to life.

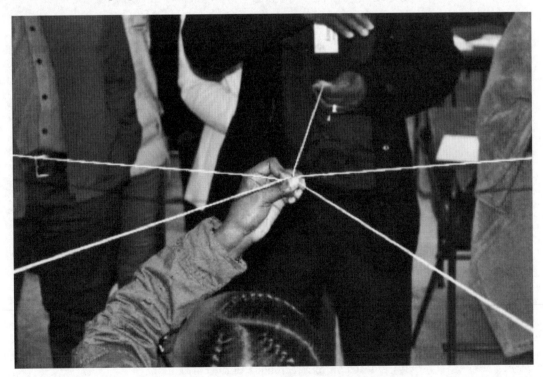

Learners hold 5 equally spaced pieces of string to show angles at centre of regular polygon. See chapter 13

Communication in the classroom

Strategies 3 to 6 are grouped around the theme of communication in the classroom. These strategies will help you to develop a whole range of teaching skills so that you will be better able to judge what your learners understand and to adjust your teaching to help them develop their understanding.

Strategy 3: Questioning

Questioning is used as a strategy in chapters 4,13 and Key questions are included in each chapter.

What sort of questions are useful and why? What type of question will encourage the learner to explain? Some workshops take questioning as the main strategy but in all workshops you will find suggestions for two or three Key Questions to use as you try to help the learners develop their mathematical thinking. See page 7.

Strategy 4: Discussion

Discussion is used as a strategy in chapters: 2, 3, 5, 10, 13, 18.

How do you get the learners to talk to each other about the mathematics? First you need an activity that is interesting enough for the learners to want to talk about it and then questions to focus the discussion. Working in pairs is often the easiest to arrange and can be very effective. See page 8.

Strategy 5: Getting feedback

Getting feedback is used as a strategy in chapters 4 and 8 and whenever the use of showboards is suggested.

Add to the ways in which you find out what the learners understand during the lesson so that you can adapt your teaching effectively. See page 10.

Strategy 6: Starting from a problem not a technique

Problem not a technique is used as a strategy in chapters: 6, 9 and whenever an activity clearly leads on to a technique in the curriculum.

Communication isn't going to work if the learners don't see the point of what they are learning. Presenting a problem that interests the learners can be used to show the need for a particular technique. See page 12.

Strategy 3: Questioning

Questions to check on knowledge and understanding (usually factual)

One way of categorising factual questions is whether they are closed or open.

A closed question has a definite answer e.g.

"What is the solution of the equation $2x + 3 = 17$?"

An open question has many possible answers e.g.

"Can you tell me an equation which has as solution $x = 7$?

Open questions can tell us much more about what learners know. They are also very economical because they allow learners to give you different possible answers, all of which can be correct! Here are some open questions that help learners to think about facts and the structure of the mathematics they are learning about.

Give me an example of a square number

What makes $x(2 + x)$ an example of a quadratic equation?

What is the same and different about 2, 4, 6, 8,10.... and 5, 7, 9, 11, 13, ... ?

What needs to be changed so that (2,4) (3, 5) (5, 10) (6, 12) are all points on the same straight line?

Questions to develop understanding

These are usually questions about thinking. It is often useful to ask learners how they worked something out, by asking questions such as How did you...? What if you....? Why did you...? The answers learners give are useful in knowing how well they understand what they are doing.

Who asks the questions?

When teachers set out to give activities to learners whereby the learners will investigate mathematical ideas and discover relationships and meanings for themselves, the teachers need to ask the right sorts of questions to guide the learners. In each workshop we suggest key questions you can use to help the learners to develop understanding and so that the teacher can judge how best to guide that individual.

Usually the teacher asks the questions and the learners give the answers. Learners should be given opportunities to ask questions as well as to answer them. Perhaps you could begin a new topic by asking the learners to write down topic questions they would like to know the answer to. At the end of a topic you could ask the learners to pose their own questions for each other. These sorts of activities can help you as a teacher to know more about what your learners know and understand.

Further reading

Mason, J. (2010) Effective Questioning and Responding in the Mathematics Classroom. mcs. open.ac.uk/jhm3/Selected%20Publications/Effective%20Questioning%20&%20Responding.pdf

Strategy 4: Discussion

A group of teachers at a workshop can use the one, two, four, more approach. Working individually at the start gives everyone time and space to read the introduction to the task and to think quietly so as to sort out their own ideas. After a few minutes it can help to work in pairs to do the activity together and to discuss it. Later if two pairs make up a foursome they may find that they have taken different approaches and have valuable ideas to exchange with the other pair. Finally each foursome will have something worthwhile to contribute to a whole group discussion.

- **One**

  At the start of the lesson, the teacher introduces a task and asks learners to spend a few minutes 'doing' the task on their own. The task should be such that everyone can make a start. This stage is important so that nobody can get the idea that they just wait for someone else to do the work, which is one of the problems that can arise with group work in class.

- **Two**

  Then, at a signal from the teacher, the learners work in pairs and 'talk' about the task. They should discuss the methods they have been using. Is anyone stuck? Can they help each other? Are they thinking the same way? Did they think of the same method or different ways of tackling the task? What can they learn from each other? They should do the task together by at least one method, record their work and check their answers. This paired work should take up at least half the lesson. Even in the largest class, with limited space, it is usually possible to organize paired work.

Paired discussion gives everyone a chance to speak

- **Four**

  When the teacher decides that the moment is right she instructs each pair of learners to work with another pair to make up a foursome. For smooth transitions the teacher may decide that the learners should sit in the same places in all the mathematics lessons, work with the same partners and make up the same groups of four. For example, if the class are not sitting around tables half the pairs might turn around to work with the pair behind them, to talk about the work they have done. Again they can compare methods and check to see if they have got the same answers or equivalent answers. Again they might try to do the task by an alternative method and record their work.

A group of four discuss a matching activity

- **More**

  This is the whole class discussion at the end of the lesson when the teacher builds on what the learners have discovered for themselves. The teacher calls on representatives of different groups to report to the whole class on how they tackled the task and what they have found out, then summarizes the ideas and perhaps adds some explanation, for example on the connections between the different approaches used or the different points of view taken.

Further reading

Ray, R. Paired and group work for secondary school learners in mathematics. School Improvement Service. East Riding of Yorkshire Council.

http://www.eriding.net/maths/tl_resources_sec.shtml

Strategy 5: Getting feedback

During a lesson a teacher needs to get as much feedback as possible on what the learners understand and how many of them are confused. A traditional method of getting feedback is to ask learners to put their hand up if they want to respond to a question. The teacher can then choose learners to answer. There are other ways of getting feedback on what learners think that enable the teacher to get more information about more learners.

Thumbs up/thumbs down

Show me thumbs up if you think this statement is true, and thumbs down if you think it is false. The teacher uses a question that can be answered by yes or no. The learners think for a moment and, at the teacher's signal, everyone show thumbs up or thumbs down. A variation is to allow learners to hold their thumbs horizontal to show they are unsure. The teacher can follow up by asking several learners to explain why they chose their response.

Disadvantage   The teacher has to think of useful yes/no questions.

Advantage   The teacher can scan the room and get some feedback about all the learners.

Individual showboards (or show-me boards)

In many countries children in primary schools use individual chalkboards to practice writing and to show teachers their answers. This traditional method is being revived in some European, Asian and African countries with some interesting variations.

- It is being used with learners of all ages from 5 to 18.
- The showboards may be chalkboards or mini whiteboards, or laminated sheets of paper with marker pens that can be rubbed out.

Graphs on showboards

Showboards are particularly useful for open questions. An open question is a question that can have many answers, for example: show me a number that is divisible by 3.

All learners can answer the question; more confident learners can give numbers such as 120, or 72000 to show their understanding. The teacher can look around the class and, to encourage discussion, can ask several learners to show their boards to the whole class or choose two boards e.g. one with an odd and one with an even number.

Another example might be: show me a sketch of a graph with a gradient of +1.

Graph with a gradient of +1

Disadvantage   The need to convince colleagues that these boards are just as valuable with older learners as with young learners and to buy or make a class set of boards.

Advantage   Each learner must be active and the teacher can quickly judge the understanding of all the learners. The boards can be used to get responses from groups in large classes.

Further reading

Standards Unit Improving learning in mathematics: challenges and strategies Malcolm Swan University of Nottingham https://www.ncetm.org.uk

Strategy 6: Starting from a problem not a technique

In the curriculum, there will be a list of topics such as: Multiplication of fractions, Solving linear equations, Angles in a triangle. This could suggest a teaching style based on a rather mechanical format.

- Stage 1   Demonstrate the technique for solving linear equations
- Stage 2   Practice the technique with a set of exercises gradually increasing in difficulty.

Syllabuses describe the solutions not the problems so the learners never get to understand WHY the techniques were developed. With teaching in this 'transmission' style, learners may be able to carry out routine procedures successfully but they will struggle with complex procedures and problem solving.

Teachers everywhere, over the centuries have developed and collected interesting problems that lead up to important curriculum topics. This makes possible a 'transformative' teaching style:

- Stage 0   Work on a problem that leads up to the technique
- Stage 1   Develop some techniques with the pupils
- Stage 2   Practice with interesting and varied problems.

This book contains many suggestions for Stage 0 work and interesting problems for Stage 2. We hope you will find some useful activities in this book that will help you to develop your teaching styles so that you can help learners to understand and enjoy their mathematics and to tackle mathematical problems with determination and confidence.

Discuss the value of this approach. Here are some statements to stimulate discussion.

Which ones do you agree with?

- I'm short of time already. I don't have time to add an additional stage.
- A few weeks after a topic my learners have forgotten everything. I have to start all over again. Approaches they would remember would be really helpful.
- If learners develop ideas for themselves, and understand why techniques work, they will not need so much revision and repetition.
- When learners come across a slightly different problem in an exam, problem-solving techniques can give them confidence in tackling it.
- I want my learners to find mathematics more satisfying.
- When teaching equations I have to teach each slightly different type of equation separately.
- I try to teach general principles that the learner can apply to many different problems.

Further reading

Murray, H., Olivier, A., Human, P. Learning Through Problem Solving, University of Stellenbosch, South Africa. www.academic.sun.ac.za/mathed

Multiples, factors and primes

Teaching strategy: Visual and People maths

Curriculum content

Recognise, classify and represent multiples, factors and prime numbers and their relationships.

Prior knowledge needed

Multiples of single digit numbers to at least 100.

Intended Learning Outcomes

At the end of this activity teachers and learners will:

- Know the vocabulary associated with multiplication, division and prime numbers
- Understand different representations of multiple, factor and prime
- Be able to make links between multiplication and division facts
- Appreciate the value of activities which introduce concepts or reinforce understanding in different ways
- Have experienced visual, auditory and kinaesthetic activities

Fact box

A factor of a number is a number that can be divided into it exactly. 5 is a factor of 15.

A multiple of a number is made from adding the number to itself over and over again. So the multiples of 7 are: 7, 14, 21, 28 ....

A number that is a multiple of two or more different numbers is called a common multiple. So 100 is a common multiple of 2, 5, 10, 20, 25 and 50.

A prime number has two factors, itself and 1. So 7 is a prime number. The first prime number is 2.

The highest common factor (HCF) is the biggest number that divides exactly into two bigger numbers. The HCF of 12 and 18 is 6.

The lowest common multiple (LCM) is the smallest number that two numbers will both divide into exactly. The LCM of 15 and 10 is 30.

Resources for this workshop

Lots of small objects, e.g. dried beans, counters; ball of string; coloured pencils; photocopies of the 1–100 grids on page 20. Each pair will need 2 grids. If possible, prepare 2 large grids for everyone to see. Have a few spare grids.

Workshop Activities for Teachers

Activity 1: Handfuls

- Lots of small objects, e.g. dried beans, counters, small stones

Pairs   *20 minutes*

Work in pairs. In turns take a handful of beans. Make as many different rectangular arrays as you can from your handful of beans. Note: **putting all the beans in one line does not count as a rectangular array.**

For each rectangle you can make (and that your partner agrees with), score one point. The person with the most points wins.

Keep a record of the numbers you have taken and the rectangles you have made. What do you notice?

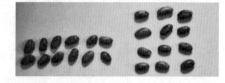

Rectangular arrays made with beans

Notes
This activity emphasises the crucial difference between prime numbers and other numbers. Prime numbers cannot be broken down into factors and so they cannot be made into any rectangular arrays. However non-prime numbers have factors and can form an array. Some non-prime numbers give lots of points. They are the numbers with lots of factors, such as 24 and 30. Initially learners may not realise that numbers like 9 and 15 can form an array and gain them a point!

Activity 2: Counting and clapping

Whole group   *20 minutes*

Try *Activity 1 Counting and clapping* on page **16** in the learner activity section.
Turn to page 16 now.

Discuss the classroom activity you have just tried. Extend the activity to four groups. (There may be just one or two teachers in each group.) Everyone together counts 1, 2, 3, 4, ... but:

Group A clap and say loudly the multiples of 2
Group B clap and say loudly the multiples of 3
Group C the multiples of 4
Group D the multiples of 5

How long will you have to clap before you get to a number that is clapped loudly by everybody? Try to predict this before clapping.

Notes
- Common multiples of 2 and 5 (10, 20, 30, 40...) will be clapped loudly by everybody.
- A number that is in only one set of multiples will be clapped loudly by one group.
- A number that is not in either set of multiples will be heard very quietly.
- Discuss the patterns if 2 and 4 are counted together, or 3 and 6.
- Which numbers are always quiet? Why?

Activity 3: Patterns on 100 grid

- 2 copies per pair of the 1–100 grids on page **20** and a few spare grids
- 2 large grids for everyone to see; coloured pencils

Pairs and whole group   *40 minutes*

On the first grid

Circle the number 2 then put a coloured line through every multiple of 2 up to 100. Is there a pattern? What do you see?

Using a different colour, circle the number 3 and put a line through all the multiples of 3.

Choose either 5 or 7 and do the same.

What do you see?

1	2	3	4	5	6	7	8	9	10
11	12	13	14	15	16	17	18	19	20
21	22	23	24	25	26	27	28	29	30
31	32	33	34	35	36	37	38	39	40
41	42	43	44	45	46	47	48	49	50
51	52	53	54	55	56	57	58	59	60
61	62	63	64	65	66	67	68	69	70
71	72	73	74	75	76	77	78	79	80
81	82	83	84	85	86	87	88	89	90
91	92	93	94	95	96	97	98	99	100

On the second grid

We shall have lots of multiples.

Circle the number 2. Put a line through every multiple of 2 up to 100.
Circle the number 3. Put a line through every multiple of 3 up to 100.
What do you notice about multiples of 4?
Circle the number 5. Put a line through all the multiples of 5 up to 100.
What do you notice about multiples of 6?
Circle the number 7. Put a line through every multiple of 7 up to 100.
What do you notice about the multiples of 8, 9 and 10?

What can you say about the **numbers that aren't crossed out**?

Notes
- You might wonder why, you don't cross out the first number of a table. That's because the numbers that aren't crossed out are the prime numbers – those that have no factors other than themselves and 1. The first numbers of some tables (2, 3, 5, 7...) are prime.

- There are lots of patterns to look for: numbers crossed out twice have two prime factors, numbers crossed out three times have three prime factors, etc.

- A Greek mathematician called Eratosthenes invented this systematic method of finding prime numbers. It is known as the Sieve of Eratosthenes. You could try extending this to numbers larger than 100.

- The String stars activity in the learner activities is also about factors. This activity needs 8 people so if you do not have enough people in your workshop you can discuss it now and plan how to use it with your learners. **Turn to page 17.**

String star with 8 points

Classroom Activities for Learners

Activity 1: Counting and clapping

Whole class	*20 minutes*

Whole class. Everyone counts 1, 2, 3, 4, 5... clapping on the multiples of **two** up to about 20 – clap and speak loudly on the even numbers. Speak softly and don't clap on the odds.

Softly don't clap	*Louder & clap*	*Softly don't clap*	*Louder & clap*	
1	**2**	3	**4**	... **20**

Now all count and clap on the multiples of **five** up to about 30 – clap and speak loudly on the multiples of five and softly on all the other numbers.

Divide into two groups. Count together: 1, 2, 3, 4, 5... 30. One group is going to clap the twos and *at the same time* the other group will clap the fives. Predict what you will **hear**. Which numbers will be loud?

Choose another pair of multiples, e.g. 3 and 7 and repeat this activity. Each time predict what you will hear before you clap and talk about it afterwards.

> **Teaching ideas**
> - The first time you try this activity it can be very confusing but repeat it so that the learners begin to spot the patterns and then they will enjoy counting further.
> - Encourage the learners to **predict**.

Activity 2: Patterns on 100 grid

• Coloured pencils	
• Each learner will need a 1–100 grid or squared paper	
Individual	*50 minutes*

Choose a colour. Circle 2 then put a line through 4, 6, 8, 10 .... These are the **multiples** of 2.

Do the rest of the multiples of 2. All these numbers have a **factor** of 2.

Circle 3 then put a line though the multiples of 3 which are 6, 9, 12, 15 ....

Do the rest of the multiples of 3. All these numbers have a *factor* of 3.

Which numbers have a factor of 2 and also a factor of 3? Get the learners to talk about this.

Circle the numbers 5 and 7 and cross out all their multiples. Circle all the numbers that are not crossed out. What can you say about these numbers? Write about three patterns that you notice.

> **Teaching ideas**
> - If you don't have 1–100 number grids for the learners to colour individually, you could do this as a whole class activity with one big sheet of paper at the front, or a hundred square displayed on an overhead projector. Alternatively, the learners could start by making their own hundred squares.
> - *Encourage discovery:* You might want to do the first part of the worksheet with the class and talk about the sort of patterns the learners notice and how these compare to the clapped patterns, especially the small numbers.
> - *Mathematical talk:* It's important to give the learners time to talk about what they notice. They may for example realise that the fours are already coloured in, so are the sixes, and the eights, etc. All of this helps them to get a 'feel' for the way numbers fit together. The key concept is that some numbers have only two factors, 1 and the number itself, and these are called prime numbers.

Activity 3: String stars

- Ball(s) of string

Whole group, pairs   *50 minutes with follow up time*

Getting started

Choose eight learners to stand in a circle. Number them 0, 1, 2, etc.

The ball of string is given to 0 and then to 1, then 2 and passed around the circle, unrolling it and pulling it taut.

Ask **what shape** has been made (octagon).

Ask '**what was the rule?**' (pass to next person/add one).

Now ask the learners to start again and pass the string from 0 to 2 to 4 and so on missing out one person each time until the string gets back to 0.

Ask **what shape** has been made (square).

Ask '**what was the rule?**' (two times table).

Record the numbers in order – 0, 2, 4, 6, 0 – somewhere where everyone can see them.

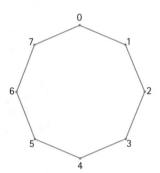

Start again

Now ask the learners to pass the string from 0 to 3 to 6 and so on until the string gets back to 0.

Ask **what shape** has been made (eight pointed star).

Ask '**what was the rule?**' (three times table).

Record the numbers in order – 0, 3, 6, 1, 4, 7, 2, 5, 0 – where everyone can see them.

Encouraging discovery

Ask the learners to draw 8 dots on a circle, number them 0 to 7 and record the patterns created in this activity.

Ask the learners to explore the patterns made using 8 dots and the 4, 5, 6 and 7 times tables.

Think, pair, share. The learners should discuss and try to explain what they notice about the patterns in pairs then as a class.

Ask the learners to draw 12 points around circles (as in a clock face), number them from 0 to 11 and investigate the different patterns they get joining points according to the different times tables.

> **Teaching ideas**
>
> The only rules that will generate stars are for numbers that do not have a **factor** in common with the number of dots. So for 8 the only stars are for the 3 and 5 times tables (which match) and for 12, only the 5 and 7 times tables (which also match) generate stars.

Changes in my classroom practice

Implementing the teaching strategy

Visual learning styles   *see page 4*
People maths   *see page 5*

All these activities emphasise the same idea that some numbers are prime, some have few factors and others have lots of factors. By doing different kinds of activities – those that work with sight, hearing and movement – around the same learning outcome we are offering all learners an opportunity to learn in the way which is most natural to them. Which way of learning do you prefer: visual, auditory or kinaesthetic? (Kinaesthetic means movement so all the People Maths activities can be described as kinaesthetic activities.) Do you think it would be useful to use these approaches more often in your teaching?

Key questions to develop understanding

Patterns on 100 grid

- 4 has three factors: 1 and 2 and 4. How many factors does 5 (or any other circled number) have?
- In colouring the Sieve of Eratosthenes, explain why using the tables up to 7 gives all the prime numbers between 1 and 100. Look carefully at the grid and explain why it is unnecessary to cross out multiples of 8, 9 or 10.
- Why is it unnecessary to cross out multiples of 11?
- If you had to find all prime numbers up to 200 using the sieve method which other multiples should you cross out?

Note: The numbers in circles have only two factors, the number itself and one.

Numbers with just two factors are called prime numbers.

1 is not a prime number as it only has 1 factor.

1	2	3	4	5	6	7	8	9	10
11	12	13	14	15	16	17	18	19	20
21	22	23	24	25	26	27	28	29	30
31	32	33	34	35	36	37	38	39	40
41	42	43	44	45	46	47	48	49	50
51	52	53	54	55	56	57	58	59	60
61	62	63	64	65	66	67	68	69	70
71	72	73	74	75	76	77	78	79	80
81	82	83	84	85	86	87	88	89	90
91	92	93	94	95	96	97	98	99	100

Handfuls

- If you have a handful of beans and you can arrange them in a rectangular pattern what does that tell you about the number of beans?
- Are all rectangular numbers even?

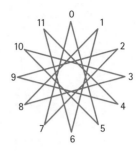

12 pointed star

String stars

- In making the 8-pointed star, did the string go to everyone? Why? (See photo on front cover of book.)
- Is there only one possible 12 pointed star? Why?

Follow up activities

You can find an interactive class version of Eratosthenes' Sieve at http://www.faust.fr.bw.schule.de/mhb/eratclass.htm.

Go to the NRICH website http://nrich.maths.org and search for these problems:

- 'Path to the Stars' Is it possible to draw a 5-pointed star without taking your pencil of the paper? Starting from this simple question your learners can explore another factors and multiples problem.
- 'Making sticks' Using cubes or strips of squared paper to explore common multiples
- 'Factors and Multiples Game' A game played on a 1 to 100 grid.

You can learn a lot from just one problem on the NRICH website. For each problem there is a menu at the side: *Problem, Getting Started, Solution, Teachers' Resources, Printable pages.*

Try the problem for yourself first so you can see what it is about. Often the initial activity seems playful and it is only when you try the activity that you can see how the mathematics emerges from the problem. Then try the other headings. *Getting Started* shows ways of starting work on the problem, *Teachers' Resources* explains why the problem is useful and *Solution* will show how some learners recorded their work on the problem.

1	2	3	4	5	6	7	8	9	10
11	12	13	14	15	16	17	18	19	20
21	22	23	24	25	26	27	28	29	30
31	32	33	34	35	36	37	38	39	40
41	42	43	44	45	46	47	48	49	50
51	52	53	54	55	56	57	58	59	60
61	62	63	64	65	66	67	68	69	70
71	72	73	74	75	76	77	78	79	80
81	82	83	84	85	86	87	88	89	90
91	92	93	94	95	96	97	98	99	100

1	2	3	4	5	6	7	8	9	10
11	12	13	14	15	16	17	18	19	20
21	22	23	24	25	26	27	28	29	30
31	32	33	34	35	36	37	38	39	40
41	42	43	44	45	46	47	48	49	50
51	52	53	54	55	56	57	58	59	60
61	62	63	64	65	66	67	68	69	70
71	72	73	74	75	76	77	78	79	80
81	82	83	84	85	86	87	88	89	90
91	92	93	94	95	96	97	98	99	100

Place value and decimal fractions

Teaching strategy: Discussion

Curriculum content

Understand number representation up to 2 places of decimals.

Add, subtract, multiply and divide numbers up to 2 places of decimals.

Prior knowledge needed

Ability to read any number including decimal numbers

Intended Learning Outcomes

At the end of this activity teachers and learners will:

- Know what the value of any digit in a decimal fraction represents
- Understand how numbers are constructed
- Be able to add, subtract, multiply and divide decimal fractions
- Appreciate the importance of being able to estimate answers
- Have experienced independent thinking

Fact box

The value of each digit in a given number depends on the position it has in the number.

Names of numbers:

500 000	– five hundred thousand
60 000	– sixty thousand
4 000	– four thousand
500	– five hundred
0.2	– nought point two (two tenths)
0.04	– nought point nought four (four hundredths)
0.007	– nought point nought nought seven (seven thousandths)

Note:

0.28 is read nought point two eight and not nought point twenty eight.

Some countries use the decimal point others use the decimal comma writing 0,28 which is read as nought comma two eight. In this book the decimal point will be used as teachers are familiar with this from calculators and computers. Any worksheets which need to be photocopied for learners will be provided in both decimal comma and decimal point form.

Resources for this workshop

Calculator for each pair of teachers; dice or card and paper-clips to make spinners. Photocopies of worksheet on page 27 (or 28 for decimal comma version). Photocopies of arrow/flard cards on pages 190 (or 189 for decimal comma version).

Workshop Activities for Teachers

Activity 1: Wipe Out

> - Calculator for each pair
>
> *Pairs*   *30 minutes*

Work in pairs.

The first person writes down a 6-digit number.

The second person keys this number into their calculator.

The first person now says: please change the digit 4 to the digit 0.
You must use the digit keys and the [−] and [=] keys

$$\boxed{745632}$$
$$\boxed{-}\ \boxed{40000}$$
$$\boxed{=}\ \boxed{705632}$$

Example: enter the number 745 632 on the calculator and try to change it to 705 632

The first person now chooses the digit 3 or 2 or 5 until they have all been wiped out (changing the original number to 0).

Now swop so that the second person chooses a number (can be more than 6 digits) and tells the first person which digits to eliminate.

Play the game again but this time the person choosing the number and the digits to be wiped out can choose 2 or more digits to be eliminated *at the same time*.

For example change 658 451 to 650 450.

Play the game again but this time choose numbers with a decimal point, e.g. 4 529.39.

> **Notes**
> - This game is designed to consolidate the concept of place value. To eliminate the 4 in 142 you need to subtract 40 and so you can see that the 4 is representing a value of 40.
> - There are many variations of this game. One variation is described in Classroom Activity 1 where learners are asked to change one number to another number using only the digit keys and the [÷] and [+] keys or the [×] and [−] keys.

Activity 2: Place the digits

- Dice or spinner with the numbers 1, 2, 3, 4, 5 and 6 for each pair. See page **192** for how to make a simple spinner

Pairs   *30 minutes*

Divide into pairs and get a dice or spinner with the numbers 1, 2, 3, 4, 5 and 6. Start with Game 1. Take turns to throw the dice or spin the spinner and each decide which of your cells to fill. Once you have written in a digit you are **not** allowed to move it.

Game 1: Addition

Each of you draw an addition grid like this:

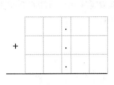

	1st player	2nd player
	2 6 . 6 1	6 3 . 6 2
+	3 5 . 1 2	5 2 . 1 5
	2 5 . 3 6	3 6 . 2 1
	8 7 . 0 9	1 5 1 . 9 8

Throw the dice or spin the spinner twelve times until all the cells are full. Each player adds up their numbers. Whoever has the sum closest to 100 wins.

Here the 1st player wins as 87.09 is closer to 100 than 151.98.

Scoring: A point for a win. The first person to reach 5 points wins the game. You can change the target to make it easier or more difficult.

Game 2: Subtraction

Same as Game 1 except now you work with a subtraction grid and your target is 1.

Game 3: Multiplication

Same as Game 1 and 2 except now you work with a multiplication grid and your target is 100.

Notes

The idea behind the game is not just to place the digits randomly but to try to place them in such a way that the answer of your addition, subtraction or multiplication sum is as close as possible to the target number. In this way you practice operations with decimal numbers and you practice estimation of calculations with decimal numbers. You will get better the more times you play the game.

Classroom Activities for Learners

Activity 1: Wipe-Out

- Photocopies of the worksheet on page **27** or **28** and cards on page **189** or **190**.
- Calculator for each pair

Pairs   *30 minutes*

Write the number 142 on the board.

Tell learners to key the number on their calculators.

Learners must now subtract a number so that they wipe out the 4 and have 102 on their calculators. (142 − 40 = 102). Now the learners must wipe out the 1 with a subtraction and finally the 2 giving 0. The number 142 has been wiped out.

Write the number 63 158.247 on the board.

Ask the learners to read the number aloud.

Tell learners to key the number on their calculators.

Ask learners to wipe out the digits one at a time using a subtraction so that they become 0 in the following order:

Wipe out 2 so the number becomes 63 158.047

then 1, followed in turn by 5, 3, 7, 6, 4, 8.

Hand out the worksheet or write the instructions on the board and allow learners to work in pairs to complete the challenges.

Teaching ideas

- This game allows learners to use trial and error and any prior knowledge of place value to consolidate their knowledge of place value and to extend it to decimal digits.

- It is important that you make sure that the learners understand that because you had to subtract 40 to eliminate the 4 in 142, the value that the 4 is representing is 40.

- You can also use arrow cards (or flard cards) to help your learners understand place value. On page **190** you will find three cards that can be used to make the number 0.473. For each digit there is a separate card that indicates the value represented by that digit.

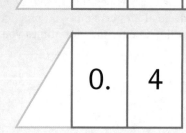

- You could start the wipe out game with the number 0.473 and ask your learners to wipe out the 7. If your learners struggle to realise that they need to subtract 0.07 you can show them the arrow cards.

- Show them how the number is built up and then how it can be broken down. Show that the 7 represents 0.07 and then ask them to try again to use their calculator to wipe out the 7 in 0.473.

Activity 2: Place the digits

- Set of ten small cards with the digits 0 to 9
- Paper and at least one calculator for each group

Pairs   *15 minutes*

Make the biggest possible 4 digit number

Ask the learners to draw 4 squares in a row. Explain that you will choose 4 digits and that they must use these digits to make the **biggest** possible 4-digit number.

Without looking, choose a card from the set of 10 cards and show the learners the card.

DO NOT replace this card.

The learners must decide where to place the digit on the card. Once the digit is placed its position cannot be changed.

Repeat for three more cards.

If the digits are 5, 1, 3, 7, then two possible arrangements are:

Group A	Group B
5 7 1 3	7 1 5 3

Group B wins one point as they have the biggest number.

The first group with 5 points wins.

Make the smallest possible 5–digit number

This time the learners must draw 5 squares. The same rules apply as the first time. The group with the smallest number wins.

If the digits are 4, 6, 1, 2, 9, 3

    Group 1 might write down: 12436

    Group 2 might write down: 14269

    In this case group 1 will win a point as they have the smallest number.

Make the closest number to 0.5

This time learners must draw 4 squares with a decimal point between the first two columns and fill in a 0 in the first column. You must choose a card 3 times. The group with the number closest to 0.5 wins.

If the digits are 7, 2, 3:

    0 . 2 3 7

    Group 1 might write down: 0.237

    Group 2 might write down: 0.723

    In this case group 2 will win a point as they have the number closest to 0.5. Sometimes a subtraction is needed to see which number is closest to 0.5

The first group to gain 5 points is the winner.

> **Teaching ideas**
>
> To let your learners get the idea of the game, let them try to get the biggest number possible a few times before moving onto the smallest number possible and then finally onto making a decimal fraction. You can make up your own numbers that you are aiming for.

Changes in my classroom practice

Implementing the teaching strategy

Discussion   *see page 8*

Games and some competition are motivating for teenagers. Whilst they are playing you will hear them discussing and talking about the mathematics. When you hear an interesting comment you can ask the pair to repeat it to the class. You have told them it is a useful comment so they can feel confident.

If they can enjoy building up their skill their learning will be better. If learners keep a record of their scores they can compete against their own previous best work.

In the first activity a game is used to consolidate a concept. Games such as the one in the second activity are useful for practising important skills (operations with decimal fractions) that might otherwise be tedious to practice.

With any game it is important that at the end of the game the teacher makes sure that all the learners have understood the concept or mastered the skill that the game was designed for.

Key questions to develop understanding

- What is the value of the 4 in 142? How can you use your calculator to show this?
- What is the value of the 4 in 156.249? How can you use your calculator to show this?
- Why is it incorrect to read 0.28 as nought point twenty eight?
- When playing the game – ask 'Why did you choose to put that number in that cell?'

Follow up activity

Using People Maths to review multiplying and dividing by 10

You will need four chairs set out at the front of the room and showboards.

Hand out showboards to learners near the front and ask them each to write a digit on their board so you have 1, 2, 3, 4, 5, 6, 7, 8, 9 and four boards with 0.

Ask learners to come and sit on the chairs to show:

- the number three thousand,
- then move to show $3000 \div 10$, then $300 \div 10$, $30 \div 10$.

How can we show $3 \div 10$?

Write a decimal point on a showboard and get a learner to stand to the right of the chairs (when you face the chairs) with the decimal point.

Place another chair to the right of the decimal point to show 0.3.

Change the number to 4.32 and then start multiplying by 10 or 100 or 1000 adding more chairs as needed.

This is a useful demonstration that multiplying by 10 sends all digits one place to the left with the decimal point fixed. Vary the activity and discuss with the class until they are quite certain that 2.3 multiplied by 10 is **not** 2.30 but 23.

Wipe-Out: a calculator game

1. Key in 4 682.736 and by using the digit keys and only the [–] and [=], change the 8 into a 0, the 3 into a 0, the two sixes into zeroes and then the 7 and the 4 simultaneously into zeroes.

2. Key in 3 749.123 and change this number into 3 040.103 in **one** step using the digit keys and the [–] key.

3. Key in 513 245.87 and change it into 412 245.86 in one step by only using the digit keys and the [–] key.

4. Key in and change to the indicated amount by using the digit keys and the [×] and [–] keys on your calculator.

   a   Key in 58.76 and change to 170.08

   b   Key in 146.24 and change to 1310.08

   c   Key in 234.07 and change to 1205.30

   d   Key in 67.123 and change to 267.512

5. Key in and change to the indicated amount by using the digit keys and the [÷] and [+] keys on your calculator.

   a   Key in 246.124 and change to 125.163

   b   Key in 2 468.128 and change to 717.134

   c   Key in 6 432.9 and change to 1 265.69

   d   Key in 67.99 and change to 6.18

Decimal point version

Wipe-Out: a calculator game

1. Key in 4 682,736 and by using the digit keys and only the [–] and [=], change the 8 into a 0, the 3 into a 0, the two sixes into zeroes and then the 7 and the 4 simultaneously into zeroes.

2. Key in 3 749,123 and change this number into 3 040,103 in **one** step using the digit keys and the [–] key.

3. Key in 513 245,87 and change it into 412 245,86 in one step by only using the digit keys and the [–] key.

4. Key in and change to the indicated amount by using the digit keys and the [×] and [–] keys on your calculator.

   a   Key in 58,76 and change to 170,08

   b   Key in 146,24 and change to 1310,08

   c   Key in 234,07 and change to 1205,30

   d   Key in 67,123 and change to 267,512

5. Key in and change to the indicated amount by using the digit keys and the [÷] and [+] keys on your calculator.

   a   Key in 246,124 and change to 125,163

   b   Key in 2 468,128 and change to 717,134

   c   Key in 6 432,9 and change to 1 265,69

   d   Key in 67,99 and change to 6,18

Decimal comma version

Links between fractions, decimals and percentages

Teaching strategy: Visual and discussion

Curriculum content

Deeper understanding of fractions, decimals, percentages and the links between them

Prior knowledge needed

First ideas about fractions, decimals, percentages, including understanding of equivalent fractions

Intended Learning Outcomes

At the end of this activity teachers and learners will:

- Know how to represent parts of a whole in a variety of ways
- Understand how pictures can show the relationships between equivalent fractions, decimals and percentages
- Be able to change between fractions, decimals and percentages in a variety of situations
- Appreciate the links between fractions, decimals and percentages
- Have experienced having to justify the links they claim

Fact box

Parts of a given whole can be labelled in different ways: as fractions, decimals or percentages, and it is useful to be able to change between these.

Depending on the situations, one representation might be easier than another.

$\frac{3}{5}$ is one of an infinite family of equivalent fractions: $\frac{6}{10}, \frac{9}{15}, \frac{12}{20}$ and so on.

$\frac{3}{5}$ can be thought of as 3 wholes shared equally among 5, or $\frac{1}{5}$ three times over.

$\frac{3}{5}$ can be worked out as $3 \div 5$ or 0.6. The first 2 decimal places give us the %, since the first 2 places tells how many $\frac{1}{100}$ths: in this case, $\frac{3}{5}$ is 60%.

To find $\frac{3}{5}$ of an amount, it's usually easiest to find $\frac{1}{5}$ of it (by dividing by 5) and then multiply that by 3 – but it might be easier to find $\frac{1}{10}$ then multiply by 6, or....

Resources for this workshop

Squared paper; showboards; scissors; sticky tape; photocopy of cards and dominoes on page 36 for decimal point version, page 191 for decimal comma version.

Workshop Activities for Teachers

Activity 1: Pictures for fractions, decimals and percentages (FDP)

- Paper (squared paper is easiest!) or showboards

Pairs   *20 minutes*

Percentages on a 10 × 10 grid

In pairs, draw a 10 × 10 grid, and shade 20% of it. Now write the fraction shaded in several different ways, e.g. 20%, 0.2, etc.

Can you think of a more interesting way to shade 20%?

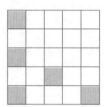

20% of a 5 × 5 grid

Percentages on other sizes of grid

Now shade 20% of a 10 × 5 grid, then 20% of a 5 × 5 grid. How would you convince learners that what you have is correct?

Shading a grid for someone else to label

One teacher draws a grid and shades part of it, for example, as shown in the picture.

Another teacher then has to label it.

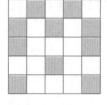

Possible labels: $\frac{10}{25}$ or $\frac{2}{5}$ or $\frac{40}{100}$ or 40% or 0.4.

Which grids are hardest, and why?

Which 'parts' are hardest? What would you do for another fraction that does not make an exact decimal or percentage?

40% of a 5 × 5 grid

> **Notes**
> Thinking about 'awkward' fractions such as $\frac{1}{3}$ is important: it's actually $33\frac{1}{3}$%, so $33\frac{1}{3}$ little squares out of 100. Using 100 squares to begin with helps learners to understand that a % is the number out of 100; moving to other size grids helps them then to get a wider understanding of percentages.

Activity 2: Making sentences about FDP

- Paper; scissors
- Photocopy of cards for each pair (page 36 for decimal point version, page 190 for decimal comma)

Pairs *30 minutes*

Each pair, cut out the cards on page 36:

0.6	$\frac{1}{5}$	$\frac{1}{3}$	200%	$\frac{1}{2}$	$\frac{1}{4}$	of	36	600	10	200	150	50
$\frac{2}{3}$	100%	25%	0.75	$\frac{1}{10}$	30%	is	100	80	500	1000	300	2000

Arrange the cards to make as many true sentences as you can, e.g. 0.6 *of* 500 *is* 300.

Can you use all the cards?

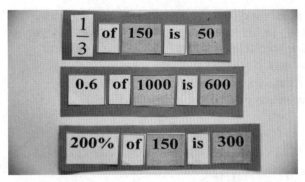

Sentences made with the cards

Activity 3: Trying classroom activities

- Showboards; scissors; sticky tape

Pairs, whole group *30 minutes*

Now try all the activities in the Classroom Activity pages 32 to 33 that you haven't tried yet.

Discuss what your learners would gain from each activity and choose the ones you will try with your learners taking into account class size and resources available. Which activity will you use first?

It is useful to spend 10 minutes at the start of a lesson on one of these activities if you know that the learners will need to use fractions, decimals and percentages in the main part of the lesson.

Classroom Activities for Learners

Activity 1: Different representations of fractions, decimals and percentages

> - Showboards or paper
>
> *Pairs or threes*   *15 minutes*

Draw a circle and put a fraction in the middle, e.g. $\frac{7}{10}$.

Draw about 6 other circles on lines out from the first. Ask each group to draw a copy of the circle diagram and fill each empty circle with either a picture of the fraction, or some words, or another fraction or decimal or percentage, that means the same as $\frac{7}{10}$.

Ask for suggestions on showboards, and make each group justify its answers. Keep asking 'does any group have something different?' Ask as many different learners as possible.

Repeat with a different fraction (harder or easier, depending on response to first fraction).

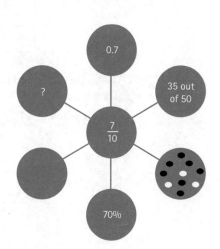

Activity 2: Pictures for fractions, decimals and percentages

> - Showboards or paper
>
> *Individual or pairs*   *20 minutes*

Shading a 10 × 10 grid

Ask the learners to draw a 10 × 10 grid, shade *any* 30 little squares and label it 30% or 0.3 or $\frac{3}{10}$ (or any other equivalent fraction). Explain that these are different names for the same part of a whole, and whichever is easiest can usually be used.

Encourage the learners to find a pattern of shading that is different to those around them.

Ask the learners to draw 3 more 10 × 10 grids and shade different percentages, e.g. 25%, 17%, 10%.

Shading a 10 × 5 grid or a 5 × 5 grid

As learners get more confident ask them to shade 0.1 of a 10 × 5 or $\frac{1}{5}$ of a 5 × 5 grid. Choose learners to come to the front of the class to explain how they know that what they have shaded is correct, and how they know that their labels are correct.

Learners are making connections between different labels for a part (fraction, decimal or percentage) and pictures of those parts.

Activity 3: Making dominoes

- Scissors; paper; showboards
- A set of 6 large paper dominoes fixed to board with sticky tape so they can be moved around (see page **36** for decimal point version, see page **190** for decimal comma version).

Whole class, groups of 3   *40 minutes*

Matching the dominoes

Use sticky tape to fix this domino on left of the board and all the other dominoes on the right. Ask the learners to look for a domino to match the $\frac{2}{5}$ and draw that domino on their showboards.

0.5	$\frac{2}{5}$

Ask a learner to come to the board and to place the matching domino as in the picture below.

0.5	$\frac{2}{5}$		40%	$\frac{3}{100}$

When the last domino is placed ask the learners to suggest a fraction or percentage to replace the ? that has the same value as the 0.5 on the first domino. So now the 6 dominos make a loop.

0.75	?

Last domino

Shuffle and repeat

Shuffle the dominoes. Choose any domino to start and see how quickly the class can form the loop.

Making your own set of dominoes

Organise the learners in groups of 3 and tell them that they are going to make their own set of dominos using fractions, decimals and percentages they choose themselves.

- The set should have at least 10 dominoes.
- The final domino **MUST** link back to the first so that the dominos form a loop. The dominoes need to form a loop so that you can start from any domino.

Help the learners to find equivalent representations to include in their dominoes.

> **Teaching ideas**
> - Make sure that learners do not put equivalent fractions on the same domino e.g. 0.4 and $\frac{2}{5}$.
>   This will make the activity impossible as different values are needed for matching other dominos.
> - Learners can be helped by putting suggestions for equivalent fractions, decimals and percentages on the board. If all the individuals use fractions and decimals from the list the whole class will have a big set of dominos to use in further classes or for playing in leisure time.
> - As you circulate ask the learners to explain how they work out their matching fractions, decimals and percentages.

Changes in my classroom practice

Implementing the teaching strategy

Visual teaching strategy	*see page 4*
Discussion	*see page 8*

By giving learners lots of different opportunities to make links between fractions, decimals and percentages, including different pictures of them, those links are made stronger so that learners can choose which is easiest to use in a given problem.

Pictures are important tools: use them with learners of all ages, and let younger learners see the pictures that older learners use, so they know that it is a good mathematical way of thinking. Ask for a representation that no one else has. This shows that you value unusual thinking.

Talking about ideas, *listening* to other learners' ideas, and *justifying* different representations, deepens understanding. Keep asking learners to *explain* how they know something is true.

Think: Which fractions turn into exact decimals? Why? Challenge your learners to find out!

Teachers listen and discuss

Key questions to develop understanding

Pictures for fractions, decimals and percentages

- So which fractions or percentages are easy to show on a 10 × 10 (or 10 × 5, or 5 × 5) grid?
- Why? What would be hard parts to show?
- How would you answer the same question using a 6 × 5 grid?

Fractions, Decimals, Percentages: Different representations

- Who has a different sort of way of showing $\frac{7}{10}$?
- Why is that equivalent?
- Does anyone have an especially interesting way of showing $\frac{7}{10}$? Convince us that it is equivalent.
- What fraction could we try that would make this activity really hard? Why?
- If we know the decimal for $\frac{1}{2}$ can we use this to find the decimal equivalent for $\frac{1}{4}$ or for $\frac{1}{8}$?

Helping learners remember

Often learners seem to understand a topic at the time of teaching but if the ideas are not used again for several weeks they will have forgotten much of what they learnt. This is the way our minds work: ideas which are refreshed and used regularly are easiest to remember. Visual reminders such as having posters up in your classroom and talking about them for a few minutes at the beginning or end of a lesson can help learners to recall important ideas. Auditory reminders such as a few minutes of mental maths will also help the memory.

Making posters for your classroom

Triples

Equivalent fractions, decimals and percentages can be displayed on a poster in the classroom. Start with some easy triples, e.g. $\frac{1}{2}$, 0.5, 50%, that will be familiar to the learners.

Over several lessons add more complex triples, e.g. $\frac{2}{3}$, 0.66, 66.6%.

Or: $\frac{1}{8}$, 0.125, $12\frac{1}{2}$%.

Include fractions larger than 1, for example, $2\frac{1}{2}$, 2.5, 250%.

Number lines

Use images showing a number line with fractions decimals and percentages all shown.

For example, make a fraction and percentage bar related to a real context like money:

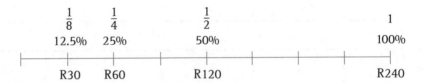

Using mental maths

In this chapter you will find activities that can be used again and again to consolidate learning of FDP. Once the learners know the activities you can use them quickly at the start of a lesson or when there are a few minutes to spare. The learners will let you know which ones they like best!

Follow up activity

Fraction, Decimal, Percentage bingo

Share out amongst the group the task of making up 25 questions about fractions, decimals and percentages with answers 1,2,3,...25. eg 1: 5% of 20, 2: $\frac{1}{4}$ of 8, 3: 0.1 of 30, 4: the number of eighths equivalent to $\frac{1}{2}$, ...

Each teacher draws a 5 × 5 grid, and places the numbers 1 to 25 on it somewhere. The grids will all be different as you can place the numbers wherever you like.

e.g.

25	7	9	3	15
16	12	24	2	11
8	18	1	19	6
5	20	23	10	13
17	21	4	14	22

One teacher now calls out questions ('clues') and the others in the group draw a line through the answer; the winner is the first to mark 5 in a straight line in any direction (in a class, you might go on until 3 learners have a line of 5).

THINK: How might you make this activity harder? Or easier? If you like the activity, how could it be adapted for other curriculum content?

0.6	$\frac{1}{5}$	$\frac{1}{3}$	200%	$\frac{1}{2}$	$\frac{1}{4}$
$\frac{2}{3}$	100%	25%	0.75	$\frac{1}{10}$	30%

of	of	of	of	of	of
is	is	is	is	is	is

36	600	10	200	150	50
100	80	50	1000	300	2000

0.5	$\frac{2}{5}$	3%	5%
0.05	$33\frac{1}{3}\%$	$\frac{1}{3}$	$\frac{3}{4}$
40%	$\frac{3}{100}$	0.75	?

Negative numbers

Teaching strategy: Questioning and getting feedback

Curriculum content

Integers. Ordering, adding and subtracting negative numbers.

Prior knowledge needed

Basic arithmetic and knowledge of the natural number line

Intended Learning Outcomes

At the end of this activity teachers and learners will:

- Know how to add and subtract positive and negative integers
- Understand the reasons for the procedures used to add and subtract integers
- Be able to use the number line to solve problems
- Appreciate the importance of negative numbers in everyday life
- Have experienced using integers to solve problems

Fact box

Integers

All positive whole numbers, negative whole numbers and zero

$$-4 \quad -3 \quad -2 \quad -1 \quad 0 \quad +1 \quad +2 \quad +3 \quad +4$$

Order of integers $^-45 < 1$
On the number line a number is less than any number on its right.

Directed numbers can be positive or negative. For positive numbers the $^+$ sign is sometimes omitted, e.g. $^-14.2$, $^-5$, 2.35, $^+34$.

Addition
Imagine the movement on a number line.
A negative number sends you left and a positive number sends you right.
If the larger movement is positive, the answer will be positive.
If the larger movement is negative, the answer will be negative.

$$(^-4) + (^+3) = (^-1) \qquad (^-4) + (^+10) = (^+6)$$

Subtraction
Subtracting a directed number is the same as adding its inverse. Subtracting a negative number sends you right on the number line.
$$(^+8) - (^-11) \text{ becomes } (^+8) + (^+11) = (^+29).$$

Resources for this workshop

Showboards or sheets of A4 paper; squared paper to draw number lines or photocopy number lines on page 193; card or paper in two different colours for extension activity on page 44.

Workshop Activities for Teachers

Activity 1: Introducing and comparing directed numbers

> • Showboards
> *Pairs, whole group*   *30 minutes*

Introducing integers

Many models can be used to introduce integers. Each of these is associated with a specific vocabulary: hot/cold, above/below and so on. All the models involve numbers that have a zero point and the idea of direction and lead to a number line with positive and negative numbers.

Model	Zero point	Adjectives	Notes
Temperature	Freezing point of water	Hot/cold	This approach is suitable in places which get cold
Altitude above or below sea level	Sea level	Above/below	Consider things above/below surface. For example, a fish 5 m below and a bird 10 m above.
The heights of a group of learners	Choose the height of a learner with a height near the median height.	Taller/shorter	Measure the heights of some learners; the height of one learner is the zero point; if she is 1 m 55 cm tall, a 1 m 60 cm pupil is $^+5$, a 1 m 45 cm learner is $^-10$.
The amount of money we have[1]	Having no money	Richer/poorer	Owing R6 is $^-6$, having R8 is $^+8$.
Time after or before a particular year	Choose a year, such as birth year of most class members or an important year.	Before/after	Any year can be taken as zero. In South Africa, 1994 is a good choice. Three years before 1994 is ($^-3$), 2015 is ($^+21$).

 Discuss these different approaches and any others that you use.

Demonstrations

 Choose someone to be the teacher and demonstrate. Decide which you think would be the best to use in your classes. Whichever one you use, start from the vocabulary – hot/cold, above/below and so on. You must stress that whatever model you use the numbers have a zero point and a direction. Draw a number line with positive and negative numbers and ask each other questions using the model you prefer.

Comparing numbers

 Use each model in turn to show why, for example, $^-45 < 1$. Learners often think this is absurd. The models should make it seem sensible.

> **Notes**
> [1] The South African currency R(Rand) is used here. Please substitute the currency your learners will be familiar with.

Activity 2: Adding and subtracting directed numbers

> • Showboards; number lines
>
> *Whole group*   *60 minutes*

- **Positive number + positive number** is a move right on the number line. This is familiar to learners.
- What about **negative number + negative number**?

  We need to show that adding a negative number is a move left. Take it in turns to present these ideas to the group using some of the models discussed in Activity 1.

  For example, (⁻3) + (⁻4) = (⁻7) can be thought of as a temperature fall of 3° followed by a fall of 4° or as owing R3 and then owing R4 more. We can show this on the number line:

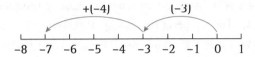

  This is 3 steps left followed by 4 steps, a total of **7** steps left.

  Note that we start from zero, not from the first number.

- **Positive number + negative number** is not so easy. But (⁺4) + (⁻5) = (⁻1) can be thought of as a temperature rise of 4° followed by a fall of 5° or as being given R4 and then owing R5. We can show this on the number line:

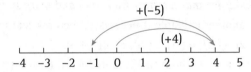

  4 steps right and then 5 steps left is 1 step left.

- Similarly for **negative number + positive number**: (⁻4) + (⁺5) is 4 steps left to −4 and then 5 steps right (⁺5) which is 1 step right.

- This leaves the problem of **number – negative number**. Does this send you right on the number line or left? Read and try for yourselves Classroom Activity 2.

  Then read the more formal explanations on pages **43 & 44** that subtracting a negative number is the same as adding its inverse.

Notes
- When adding a positive and negative number, the answer can be positive or negative; this will depend on the size of the numbers you start with.
  - So (⁻4) + (⁺6) = (⁺2) is positive because 6 > 4, and the larger 6 is positive.
  - But (⁺4) + (⁻6) = (⁻2) is negative because the larger 6 is negative.
- The quick way to add (⁻108) + (⁺110) is to note that the difference between 108 and 110 is 2. The larger number 110 is positive so the answer is ⁺2. (⁺108) + (⁻110) = ⁻2, because 110 is negative. Using the number line will help learners to develop this approach for themselves.

Classroom Activities for Learners

Activity 1: Adding directed numbers

- Showboards; number lines on strips of paper or drawn in books

Whole class, pairs   *50 minutes*

Adding integers using a number line

- Introduce learners to the number line using the model you prefer from Teachers Activity 1. Show that adding a negative number is a move left. Use showboards to get feedback.
- **Start with 'negative number + negative number'**
  Ask: "The temperature falls by 3° then by 4°. What is the total fall?" *Answer* 7°.
  Ask: "I owe R3, then I owe R4 more. What is my total debt?" *Answer* R7.
  Write (⁻3) + (⁻4) = (⁻7) and show 3 steps left followed by 4 steps left on the number line:

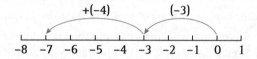

Emphasise that we start from zero and move to the first number.
Do another example if necessary; then ask learners to try some with the number line:
a (⁻2) + (⁻3); **b** (⁻1) + (⁻5); **c** (⁻4) + (⁻5).
Then some without the number line: **d** (⁻13) + (⁻41); **e** (⁻3.6) + (⁻18.2).

- **Then 'positive number + negative number'** and **'negative number + positive number'**
  Ask: "The temperature rises 4° then falls 5°. What is the change?" *Answer* A fall of 1°.
  Write (⁺4) + (⁻5) = (⁻1) and show this on the number line:

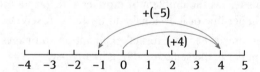

4 steps right and then 5 steps left is 1 step left.
(⁻6) + (⁺7) is 6 left, then 7 right which is 1 step right.
Learners in pairs try: **a** (⁻2) + (⁺3); **b** (⁺1) + (⁻5); **c** (⁻4) + (⁺8); **d** (⁻4) + (⁺4); **e** (⁻36) + (⁺18)

Activity 2: People Maths: Subtracting a negative number

- Showboards or paper with large numbers written on

Whole group, individual   *50 minutes*

Write these numbers on showboards or paper large enough to be seen at the back of the class. Ask 7 learners to stand at the front holding up the numbers.

Have four learners sitting down with more numbers on showboards: .

Ask the class to add up the numbers and show the answer on showboards or paper.
Write on the board. **The total is 10.**

- **Adding a positive number.**

  Ask the learner sitting down with number 3 to join the line at the front.

  Ask class to thumbs up if they think the total will go up, thumbs down if they think the total will go down. Add the numbers again. The **total** has gone up to 13.

  So adding a positive number makes total go up.

  Back to the starting position: number 3 must sit down again so total is again 10.

- **Adding a negative number.**

  Now ask negative 2 to join the line and repeat. The **total** will go down to 8. Number –2 sits down again so total is again 10.

- **Subtracting a positive number.**

  Now subtract positive 2 by asking ⁺2 to sit down so the total again goes down to 8!

  Conclusion 1: 'ADD negative 2' has exactly the same effect as 'SUBTRACT positive 2.'

- **Subtracting a negative number.**

  Ask the –3 to sit down, the total goes up to 13.

  Conclusion 2: 'SUBTRACT –3' has same effect as 'ADD positive 3.'

  So ⁺10 – (⁻3) = ⁺10 + (⁺3) = 13.

  Record in a table:

Starting total		Final total
10	ADD ⁺3	13
10	SUBTRACT ⁻3	13
10	SUBTRACT ⁻6	16
10	ADD ⁺6	16

So to subtract a negative number you go right on the number line.

You will probably need to repeat the activity above until the learners gain confidence.

Try some mental maths problems with answers on showboards.

Changes in my classroom practice

Implementing the teaching strategy

Questioning	*see page 7*
Getting feedback	*see page 10*

Discuss which of these ideas you will use:

Dramatic teaching style

Explaining operations on negative numbers needs all your teaching skills. Involve the learners. Get the learners to use their thumbs to show whether you are moving right or left on the number line. Mark a number line on the floor and pace right and left yourself or get the learners to move.

Using showboards to get feedback

How will you know if your learners (all the learners!) understand? This is a topic where it is particularly crucial for the teacher to get feedback on who understands and who needs more explanation. Providing a class set of showboards and a supply of pens is probably the simplest single thing your school can do to improve the quality of teaching. If you don't have showboards then try to acquire a good supply of scrap paper so that the learners can display their answers to you by holding up the paper. You can make a very effective showboard by photocopying the square grid on page 100 and laminating the sheet of paper. But you will still need to get hold a supply of dry-erase pens. Regular use of the showboards will help you to gather the information you need for formative assessment.

Number Line

It is helpful to have a number line from −10 to +10 on permanent display above the board. The learners can also have a number line strip or a carefully drawn number line at the back of their book.

Emphasising the idea of inverse

Include examples in which integers are added to their inverses. For example, $(^-4) + (^+4) = 0$ and 4 left followed by 4 right on the number line takes us back to 0. Being very familiar with inverses will be helpful when trying to understand subtracting a negative.

Errors and misconceptions

It's a lot simpler to just teach the learners that 'two minuses make a plus' – what's wrong with that?

Some of the most deep-seated misconceptions come from children learning something that is partially true and then applying it to other situations where it is not true. This is called *overgeneralising*.

For example, in Grade 5 a learner may solve problems like 57×10 by remembering that to multiply by 10 you add a zero. This is marked correct by the teacher and the learner feels good. In Grade 8, $5.7 \times 10 = 5.70$ is marked wrong and the learner feels confused and upset that what was perfectly acceptable before is now rejected.

'To multiply by 10 you add a zero' only works for whole numbers. It is much safer to teach learners the slightly more cumbersome method of multiplying by 10 by keeping the decimal point fixed and moving the digits one place to the left. This is how decimal numbers are designed so it always works for whole numbers and decimals.

For negative numbers the dangerous phrase is 'two negatives make a positive'. This is vague and can lead to learners overgeneralising and applying when all they can see is two negative signs

e.g. $-4 + ? = -10$ is answered as 6.

It is true that **a negative number multiplied by a negative number gives a positive number** and that **a negative number divided by a negative number gives a positive number.**

It is true that **subtracting a negative number is the same as adding a positive number.**

$-(^-2)$ is the same as $+(^+2)$

Misconceptions often turn up when learners apply the ideas of negative numbers in other topics. Look out for errors in solving equations, ask the learners why and they will often quote two minuses make a plus as justification!

Follow up activities

Understanding negative numbers particularly the idea of subtracting a negative number is difficult for many learners. It is useful for teachers to know several different approaches so the follow-up activities describe a formal approach and a practical approach using cards.

Formal explanation of subtracting a negative number

Many learners are confused when trying to subtract a negative number. Classroom Activity 2 will help the learners to understand that subtracting an integer has the same effect as adding its inverse. Here is another way of explaining. Read the statements aloud slowly and don't move on until you can say – I get that!

What is $248 - 248$?   Answer 0   Why?   Because any number minus itself $= 0$

A   What is $(^-4) - (^-4)$?   Answer 0   Why?   Because any number minus itself $= 0$

B   What is $(^-4) + (^+4)$?   Answer 0   Why?   Four steps left. Four steps right.

So comparing statements A and B both start with $(^-4)$ and have an answer of 0.

So the action $- (^-4)$ in A has the same effect as $+ (^+4)$ in B.

This works for any number:

$(^-48) - (^-48) = 0$ and $(^-48) + (^+48) = 0$ so $- (^-48)$ has the same effect as $+ (^+48)$.

A few examples like this make clear that **subtracting a negative number is the same as adding a positive number.**

To subtract a negative number you move right on the number line.

Note on formal notation

Many people distinguish between the symbols for operations and numbers. They use '+' for adding and '–' for subtracting but raised symbols for the numbers. For example, $(^+4)$ read as 'positive 4' and $(^-3)$, read as 'negative 3'. We will do this but when you are teaching do not make a fuss and do not expect learners to distinguish the two.

Model using cards for subtracting a negative number

The number line is an extremely useful model but you may like to use this alternative model when revising or when learners get stuck. For this you will need some small cards, blue ones labeled +1, red ones labeled -1.

Each group is given six blue cards labelled +1, six red ones labelled -1.

The key idea is that the sum of one (+1) card and one (-1) is 0. They cancel each other out.

"What is a rise of 1 followed by a fall of 1?" No change (+1) + (-1) = 0.

Try the calculation (+5) + (-4) using cards.

Learners put down five (+1) cards to show (+5), and four (-1) cards for (-4).

Ask: "How many pairs of cards cancel each other?" "How many cards are left?"

Four (-1) cards cancel four (+1) cards leaving one (+1), so (+5) + (-4) = (+1).

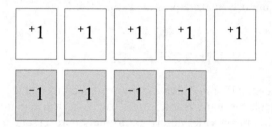

Now try these using cards: **a** (-1) + (+4); **b** (+2) + (-4); **c** (-4) + (+6); **d** (-3) + (+3); **e** (-16) + (+28).

Working without equipment. Look at your answers to the exercises. Can you see how to work out the answer without using equipment? What are: **a** (-11) + (+42); **b** (+21) + (-46); **c** (-46) + (+46); **d** (-327) + (+329)?

Subtracting negative numbers

Ask: What is (-8) - (-5)?   Set out eight (-1) cards, take away 5 (-1) cards leaves 3 (-1) cards.

Ask: What is (-5) - (-5)?   Set out five (-1) cards. Take them all away and **record** what you have done (-5) - (-5) = 0.

A problem. Set out five (-1) cards.

The problem is to get the SAME result as before – an answer of zero by ADDING cards.

Adding five (+1) cards will work! **So subtracting a negative number is the same as adding a positive number.**

Ratio and proportion

Teaching strategy: Discussion

Curriculum content

Solve problems involving proportion

Prior knowledge needed

Multiply and divide fractions and decimals. Some mental maths activities to review equivalent fractions and multiplication of fractions would be a useful starter.

Intended Learning Outcomes

At the end of this activity teachers and learners will:

- Know that there are formal and informal methods to solve proportional problems
- Understand how to spot a multiplier between two sets
- Be able to use proportional reasoning as a problem solving tool.
- Appreciate that there is more to proportion than just doubling and halving numbers
- Have used their own strategies in applying proportional reasoning to practical contexts

---

Fact box

The ratio of white to red circles is 3:2.

For every 3 white circles there are 2 red circles.

Proportional sets
When we can pair up two sets of numbers so that each pair is in the same ratio we say the sets are in proportion.

The ideas of proportion are used in many mathematical topics such as similarity, enlargement and the comparison of any two sets of numbers, for example if you can find a single multiplier to get you from each number to its pair then the sets are in proportion.

Weight of apples	(kg)	2	3	4	5	10
Price	(R)	30	45	60	75	150

The multiplier for each pair is 15. $2 \times 15 = 30$, $3 \times 15 = 45$, etc.

A multiplier is the number that you are multiplying by or the multiplying number e.g. For 130×2, the number 2 is the multiplier.

A scale factor is the number used as the multiplier in scaling usually in 1, 2 or 3 dimensions. We can scale shapes up (make the shape bigger) or scale shapes down (make the shape smaller).

The reciprocal of 4 is $\frac{1}{4}$. The reciprocal of $\frac{3}{7}$ is $\frac{7}{3}$.

Resources for this workshop
Calculators

Workshop Activities for Teachers

Activity 1: Finding the error

> • Calculators allowed
>
> *Pairs and whole group*   *50 minutes*

Here are two activities with their corresponding answers in the boxes below. Some of the answers are incorrect. Work in pairs to mark the answers.

Discuss the errors. The aim is to work out why some of the answers are incorrect rather than focusing on getting the correct answer.

Discuss how you could advise a learner to correct the error.

What is incorrect and why? How can I guide the learner to rectify the error by asking questions rather than giving the correct answer? What strategies did the learner use for each question? Are there more efficient ways of answering the question even if the answer is correct?

Mama's pancakes recipe for 4 pancakes

1 egg

1 pinch of salt

6 tablespoons of cake flour

$\frac{1}{4}$ l of milk

a) To make 8 pancakes, how much flour do I need? How much milk do I need?

b) To make 10 pancakes, how much flour do I need? How much milk do I need?

Check these answers

Which are right and which are wrong?

a) Flour: 12 tablespoons,

   Milk: $\frac{1}{4} + \frac{1}{4} = \frac{1}{8}$

b) Flour: 6 + 6 + 3 = 15 tablespoons,

   Milk: $\frac{1}{4} + \frac{1}{4} + \frac{1}{2} = 1$

Bags of rice

Calculate the missing prices in Rands (R) of the bags of rice if rice costs R30 per kilo.

0.6 kg	0.75 kg	1 kg	2.5 kg	4.25 kg
R...	R...	R30	R...	R...

Check these answers

Which are right and which are wrong?

1 kg costs R30.

4 kg costs 4 × R30 = R120,
so 4.25 kg costs R120 + R30 = R150.

2.5 kg costs R60 + R60 + R30 = R150.

$\frac{3}{4}$ kg costs $\frac{3}{4}$ of 30 $= 3 \times \left(\frac{1}{4} \text{ of } 30\right)$
$= 3 \times$ R7.50
$=$ R22.50

6 kg costs 6 × R30 = R180,
so 0.6 kg costs R18.0.

Notes

- Each question involves two quantities: e.g. the quantity of the rice and the cost of the rice. These examples help to introduce proportional sets (*a*, *b*), i.e. (quantity of rice, cost of rice). Can you think of any other proportional sets (*a*, *b*) in everyday life?

- Prices are in South African Rand – you can adapt the problem to any currency with which your learners will be familiar.

- For the recipe problem informal methods of doubling and halving work well. It makes sense to find the amount of milk for 10 pancakes by adding the amount for 4 pancakes, 4 more pancakes and 2 pancake. The method of finding the cost of one unit by dividing by 4 and multiplying by 10 is useful.

- A problem arises in the rice question when learners need to find the cost of 0.6 kg and informal methods are harder to find. The next activity will show how you can help learners with this problem in an imaginative way.

Activity 2: From 3 to 7 using only multiplication and division

- No calculators allowed

Pair and whole group   *30 minutes*

1. a) How can you get from 3 to 7 using only multiplication and division?

   Discuss in pairs.

   Record the responses on the board. There should be more than one response given. Do not discuss as a group until you have a good range of examples on the board.

   b) Whole group discussion. *Did you find lots of different ways? Were different recording methods used? Were any errors made?*

   c) Repeat the activity using only multiplication and division to get from 7 to 3.

   Try with other integers. Finding different methods makes the activity more interesting.

   What are inverse operations?

2. In this table **a** is proportional to **b**. (a, b) is a proportional set.

a	b
3	7
4	x
6	14
8	y
10	$23\frac{1}{3}$
20	z

Complete the table by finding the unknowns x, y and z:

The multiplier is $\frac{7}{3}$.

Notes

1. a) & b)   Typical responses may be $(3 \div 3) \times 7$, $(3 \times 7) \div 3$, $3 \times \frac{7}{3}$

   Perhaps written differently as $3 \rightarrow \boxed{\times 7} \rightarrow \boxed{\div 3} \rightarrow 7$

   c)   Some possible answers: $(7 \div 7) \times 3$, $(7 \times 3) \div 7$, $(7 \times 30) \div 70$, $7 \times \frac{3}{7}$

2. We call $\frac{b}{a}$ the **multiplier** or **scale factor**. Emphasise that the multiplier is constant (the same) throughout. Discuss proportional sets you have come across in everyday life.

Classroom Activities for Learners

Activity 1: Find the link

> - Calculators allowed
>
> *Pair and whole group*   *60 minutes*

Set A is 1, 2, 3, 4, 5, ..., ..., ... Set B is 2, 4, 6, 8, 10, ..., ..., ... Set C is 3, 6, 9, 12, 15, ...,

Write these sets of numbers on the board. Work with the whole class using showboards if possible.

What types of numbers are in Set A?

Can you predict the next few numbers?

Convince me how to get to the next number.

Does anyone have a different way?

Do the same for Sets B and C with the learners.

Discuss in pairs: *When you get to 100 in Set A what number will be in Set B? When you get 100 in set B what will be in set C?*

Set A	Set B	Set C
1	2	3
2	4	6
3	6	9
4	8	12
5	10	15

Can you find relationships between Set A and Set B, Set A and Set C, Set B and Set C.

Reinforce relationships between sets. Begin to focus on the usefulness of multiplication. More emphasis should be placed on Set B to Set C.

Now do Activity 2 part1 from the workshop: *How can you get from 3 to 7 using only multiplication and division?*

> **Teaching ideas**
>
> This activity encourages learners to move from additive to multiplicative relations.
>
> - Allow the learners to share their ideas on the board. If they used a combination including addition and subtraction, continue to write it on the board without giving comments. Ask the learners to describe their operation in their own words. Look out for two step operations and circle them. Do these answer the question? Eliminate the ones that do not include multiplication and division. If there are none, pose the question again. Their methods may be informal but they will be beginning to think about relationships between numbers, in particular multiplicative relationships.
>
> - Encourage the learners to think about how they could represent this multiplicative relationship. You may want to talk about dividing by 3 to get to 1 then multiplying by 7 to get 7. In other words $\div 3 \times 7$ which can also be written as $\times \frac{7}{3}$.
>
> - Allow learners to try their own sets of numbers and to choose the correct multiplier. Encourage the use of mathematical language, e.g. multiplier and scale factor. Multiplication and division are inverse operations.

Activity 2: Learning about proportion by marking scripts

> - Large sheets of paper, e.g. A3
> - Calculators allowed
>
> *Pairs or threes*   *60 minutes*

Ask each group to answer the two questions in Activity 1 of the teacher workshop. **Do not** give the learners the answers from the workshop activities for teachers, because they will look for mistakes in each other's work. The role of the teacher is to listen carefully to the learners' strategies and to facilitate participation of all learners in the group. The group should agree their method of choice and record it on a large sheet of paper including their **method.**

Choose at least two scripts at random, with correct and incorrect answers for each question, and record their methods exactly as it is on the board. Allow the groups to have a discussion about each script. The learners may choose to write down their comments on a large sheet of paper.

Ask the learners to classify which of the solutions are correct and which are incorrect. For the correct answers they should discuss the efficiency of the methods. For the incorrect answers, they should identify the errors and write strategies to improve the work. They should also write their choice of solution to share with the rest of the class.

During the whole class feedback, ask the learners: What did you think about the methods used? What kind of feedback did you think would be useful? How did you feel about discussing other learners' work? Ensure the learners have answered and agreed on these questions.

Teaching ideas
- Make links with proportional reasoning in other strands of mathematics and allow learners to give examples of proportional thinking in their everyday lives. Always refer back to the multiplier and its inverse as the important feature of proportional sets.
- Less efficient methods may help in some cases but not others. The multiplier is less intuitive but can be used for any numbers.

Changes in my classroom practice

Implementing the teaching strategy

Discussion	*see page 8*

This is a difficult topic to teach and teachers may tend to show rules for finding the multiplier without the learners understanding the concept of it. In these activities the learners are given something to discuss by making connections in two ways.

Connections with real life

Adapting the quantities in a recipe or deciding whether a larger packet is better value than two smaller packets are everyday problems but there are many other opportunities for using local resources.

Examples:

- For building, concrete and sand need to be mixed in particular proportions for safety. If the proportion is 7 to 1 how much sand is needed for 10 tonnes of concrete?
- Livestock feed often includes several ingredients mixed in specific proportions for the well-being of the animals at the most economic rate.

Connections within mathematics

The operations of multiplication and division are closely related to fractions. For example, dividing by 3 and multiplying by 7 can be achieved in one step by multiplying by $\frac{7}{3}$.

Managing discussion in the classroom

Standing at the front of the class and asking learners to discuss is unlikely to get much response until your learners are really used to talking about mathematics. So how do you get started? Many of the activities in this book are designed for pairs of learners to work on together. The learners have to be active designing a poster, solving a puzzle or trying to get the most points in a game. Once they are talking you can listen to try to understand their thinking and use what you hear to inform your teaching.

When working with the whole class you want them to have an opinion, to get involved. You can't expect the learners to make speeches but you can expect them to make simple decisions. Is this answer right or wrong? Learners can respond with thumbs up or thumbs down. If they are right they will be pleased, if wrong they may then listen more carefully to your explanation!

To get the learners' answers to a wide range of questions you could have showboards available regularly in your classroom. The answers you see on the showboards will give you a lot of information about what the learners understand. Mistakes can be rubbed out and the learning can start.

Key questions to develop understanding

- Do you think that is right? Why?
- What do you have to multiply by? Does that work for ALL the pairs?
- What do you know? What do you need to find out?

Follow up activity

Discussion of textbook problems

As your learners get used to talking about their mathematical thinking you can get them to discuss textbook style problems. Give just a few quite difficult problems and lots of time. The learners will gain just as much as from doing lots and lots of questions without so much thinking. Encourage different methods and ask the learners to explain their methods. If you notice when a learner who is not often successful has a good solution and get them to explain it you can really boost their confidence.

1. Abdul and Thandi received the same mark for their examination. They were allowed to re-sit the examination to improve their mark. Abdul obtained $\frac{5}{8}$ more than his original mark while Thandi obtained $\frac{2}{3}$ more than her original mark. Who obtained the higher final mark? How did you work out your answer?

2. A farmer sold R560 worth of apples at the local market. This pie chart shows all the things he sold. Estimate how much money he sold his strawberries for?

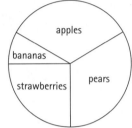

3. 10 kg of maize was sold for R16 in South Africa in 2010 when maize production was at its peak. Fill in the missing numbers. You **must** share your methods with other learners and give reasons for your choice of method. Agree on the most efficient method to work out the answers. How could you work out any amount in one step?

Amount in kilograms (kg)	10	1000	5			23	$5\frac{1}{2}$
Cost in Rands (R)	R16			R32	R2.40		

Notes
Here are some of the stages the learners might go through. If they are stuck encourage one of the pair to read the question aloud whilst the other underlines the important information.

Ask: *What do you know? What do you need to find out?*

Question 1
Understanding the question: Need to know if $\frac{5}{8}$ is bigger than $\frac{2}{3}$

Methods of solution: Could solve it visually by drawing a diagram and shading. Need to realise that drawing $8 \times 3 = 24$ boxes would make it easy to shade $\frac{5}{8}$ and $\frac{2}{3}$.

Alternatively could change both fractions to the LCD that is 24 again.

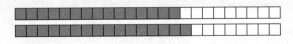

$\frac{5}{8} = \frac{15}{24}$ and $\frac{2}{3} = \frac{16}{24}$. That is close – $\frac{2}{3}$ is bigger but only just!

Question 2

There doesn't seem to be any information in this question except that R560 of apples were sold but the pie diagram provides a lot of information. Strawberries look like a quarter. The apples look like a third. So $\frac{4}{12}$ is R560 and we want to know $\frac{3}{12}$. Problem is nearly solved.

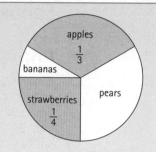

Question 3

This looks tricky. Oh, 100 kilograms is easy. It is just 16 × 100 that is 1600 and 5 is half of 10 so that must be R8.

The important thing with this type of question is to get started. The more information you have the easier the next stage is. It is easier for learners discussing the mathematics and sharing their thinking to keep trying. If you are working individually it is easier to give up.

Teachers discussing a problem

From words to algebraic expressions

Teaching strategy: Starting from a problem not a technique

Curriculum content

Writing algebraic expressions. Using brackets. Inverse operations.

Prior knowledge needed

Mental calculation

Intended Learning Outcomes

At the end of this activity teachers and learners will:

- Know how to write algebraic expressions
- Understand that brackets are used to make the meaning of algebraic expressions clear
- Be able to construct algebraic expressions from verbal descriptions
- Use the idea of an inverse
- Have experienced inventing a mathematical puzzle

Fact box

Inverse operations: addition and subtraction are inverse operations
multiplication and division are inverse operations.

Brackets are used to make the meaning of an expression clear.

For example, $(4 + 4) \div (4 + 4)$ will give a different result from $4 + (4 \div 4) + 4$ although all the same symbols are used for both expressions. The brackets tell you which parts to work out first.

Writing algebraic expressions
Unknown numbers are often represented by n or x but can also be written as a, b or any letter.

Using n to represent the unknown number:
An unknown number plus 10 can be written as $n + 10$.

In algebraic expressions the multiplication symbol ' $\times$ ' is often left out.
Double a number and add one can be written as $2n + 1$.

For some expressions a bracket is needed to make the meaning clear.
Add one to a number and then double it can be written as either as $(n + 1) \times 2$ or as $2(n + 1)$.

The bracket shows that *Add one to a number* is the first thing to happen. Then *multiply by 2*.

Resources for this workshop
Large sheets of paper; coloured pens; at least one scientific calculator; counters; four identical small boxes which will hold a few counters.

Workshop Activities for Teachers

Activity 1: Brackets first – Four fours puzzle

- Large sheets of paper; coloured pens; at least one scientific calculator

Individuals then pairs   *45 minutes*

Puzzle

First work out $(4 + 4) \div (4 + 4)$ and $4 + (4 \div 4) + 4$

(Remember to work out the brackets first!)

Talk about why each expression gives a different result.

Using four 4s and any mathematical symbols you like try to make all the numbers from 1 to 20. You **must use all four 4s.**

So, for example, to get the numbers 1 and 9

$(4 + 4) \div (4 + 4) = 1$ and $4 + (4 \div 4) + 4 = 9$.

Write the numbers from 1 to 10 on a sheet of paper and fill the answers in as you work them out.

1. $(4 + 4) \div (4 + 4)$

2.

3.

You may find more than one way for some of the numbers.

Discussion

Do you expect your learners to be confident in using brackets?

Discuss how you can help learners to use brackets correctly to get the exact expression they want.

Notes
- What mathematical symbols can be used?

  Usually everyone agrees that $+$, $-$, $\times$, $\div$ and brackets and $\sqrt{}$ can be used.

  Using $\sqrt{}$, $\sqrt[3]{}$ and ^{2} can cause more discussion. Should this be allowed?

  You as a group of teachers working on the problem can make your own decisions. If someone suggests a symbol not yet used, for example $4! = 4 \times 3 \times 2 \times 1$, make a democratic decision as to whether you will allow it. If you allow only a very few symbols the task will be harder.

- After half an hour there may still be a few numbers for which no solution has been found.

  Don't worry. The unsolved numbers can be left. The next day someone is almost certain to have come up with a solution and circulated it.

- A scientific calculator can be useful for checking if brackets are needed to get the answer you want. Allow just one person to use a calculator for checking, the mental calculation is important!

Activity 2: From words to algebraic expressions

- Counters; four identical small boxes which will hold a few counters

Whole group then pairs   *45 minutes*

Whole group

Choose someone to act as teacher and read out these instructions.

- Think of a number less than 10. Do **not** tell anyone else your starting number
- Double the number
- Add seven
- Take away three
- Divide by two
- Take away the number you first thought of.

The teacher reads the instructions then asks everyone in turn to say their final number.

The teacher then asks everyone in the group to say their starting number so everyone realises that different starting numbers were used but the final answers were all the same.

Why are the final numbers all the same?

In pairs

Turn to Classroom Activity 2 on page **56**. This shows how to use a box containing counters (or stones) to represent the unknown number. Read this now and then think how you would use drawing boxes and algebra to demonstrate this puzzle.

Think of a number. Add 2. Multiply your answer by 3. Subtract 3. Divide by 3.

Take away the number you first thought of.

Choose a pair to demonstrate with boxes and counters for the whole group.

In pairs

Try to invent a similar problem. You could start by drawing the boxes to show:

Think of a number. Add 1. Multiply by 2.

Now add a number (drawing the boxes and counters each time) and then try to undo everything.

Somehow everyone must be brought back to the same answer. That means getting rid of the boxes.

When a pair has invented a problem they can read it out for the whole group to see if everyone gets the same answer.

> **Notes**
> - The activity is based on inverse operations. An inverse operation undoes the operation and gets you back to where you started.
> - If you put your socks on and then take your socks off, you are back where you started so these are inverse operations. If you stand up and then sit down you are back where you started so these are inverse operations.
>   - *Divide by 2* is the inverse of *Multiply by 2*
>   - *Subtract 3* is the inverse of *Add 3*
>   - *Take away the number you first thought of* is the inverse of *Think of a number*
> - To invent a puzzle, first multiply and add some counters. Then try to get rid of all the boxes so you have only counters left. See page 59.

Classroom Activities for Learners

Activity 1: Using brackets with numbers – Four fours puzzle

> - A large sheet of paper and marker pen; A4 paper; sticky tape; a scientific calculator
>
> *Pairs*   *40 minutes*

Using four 4s and any mathematical symbols you like, try to make all the numbers from 1 to 20. Tell the learners they must use all four 4s and show them examples to get the numbers 1 and 8:

$$(4 + 4) \div (4 + 4) = 1 \quad \text{and} \quad (4 \div 4) \times (4 + 4) = 8$$

Ask each pair of learners to write the numbers from 1 to 20 on a sheet of paper and fill in the answers as they work them out. They can fill the numbers in any order.

> **Teaching ideas**
> - This activity requires learners to use brackets and symbols. It helps them to realise the importance of brackets in making an expression exactly as they want it to be.
> - After the learners have had some time to work on the problem, write 1 to 20 on the board and ask some of the learners to fill in their solutions. Allow plenty of space for more than one possible answer. If a large sheet of paper and marker pens are available the results can be displayed on the wall and kept for the next lesson. Have some sticky tape ready so you can tape a correct solution over any suggestions that don't work. At the end of the activity ask the learners to make a note of any numbers that have not yet been made.

Activity 2: Think of a number

> - Two or three identical boxes; counters or small objects; showboards
>
> *Whole group*   *20 minutes*

Ask everyone to think of a number less than 10 but to keep their starting number secret.

Slowly reads out these instructions, pausing to give the learners time to work it out:

- Double the number
- Add five
- Take away one
- Divide by two
- Take away the number you first thought of. This gives your final number.

Ask several learners to tell you their final number. If learners have showboards they can all write their final number on the boards and everyone can show together. Pretend to be surprised when everyone says the same number.

If someone says the wrong answer just ask lots more learners. The learner who has made an arithmetic slip will realise and probably say that they now have an answer of 2.

Ask them what number they thought of first so everyone realises that different starting numbers were used but the final answers were all the same. Hopefully the learners will be surprised and you can then show them how useful mathematics is in explaining the puzzle.

Teacher demonstrates how mathematics can explain the puzzle

First demonstration. To help the learners understand you will need two identical boxes containing a few counters and 5 extra counters. Read out the instructions in column 1 and do the actions in column 3.

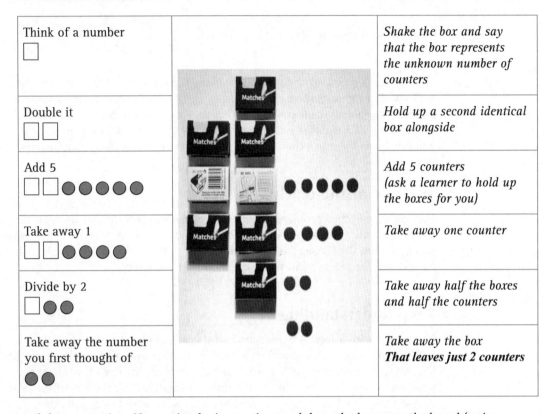

Think of a number		*Shake the box and say that the box represents the unknown number of counters*
Double it		*Hold up a second identical box alongside*
Add 5		*Add 5 counters (ask a learner to hold up the boxes for you)*
Take away 1		*Take away one counter*
Divide by 2		*Take away half the boxes and half the counters*
Take away the number you first thought of		*Take away the box* ***That leaves just 2 counters***

2nd demonstration. Now write the instructions and draw the boxes on the board (as in column 1). Give the boxes and counters to two learners and ask them to hold up the boxes and the counters as you write.

3rd demonstration. Work through the instructions on the board again but this time write n instead of a box and use numbers instead of counters

Think of a number	n
Double it	$2n$
Add 5	$2n + 5$
Take away 1	$2n + 4$
Divide by 2	$n + 2$
Take away the number you first thought of	2

Mathematics has solved the puzzle. It is not magic that everyone has the same answer it is mathematics!

Changes in my classroom practice

Implementing the teaching strategy

| *Starting from a problem not a technique* | *see page 12* |

The teacher is trying to engage and motivate the learners by encouraging them to start from a problem that interests them rather than starting with the teacher explaining a technique. In the Four fours problem the learners find that they need to use brackets to make the meaning clear. In the Think of a Number problem the learners use a symbol to stand for the unknown number and this helps them to explain the puzzle and even invent their own puzzles.

The role of the teacher

The teacher selects a problem and then gives the learners time to work on the problem. The teacher will ask the learners to explain what they are thinking rather than telling them what to do. Writing the learners' ideas on the board can be helpful. The teacher will support and encourage. The teacher will try to question rather than explain.

Deep understanding

If you start with a formal expression using symbols and then try to explain it to learners they start by not understanding and so are liable to think that mathematics is difficult. In this lesson the learners start with a puzzle which involves the use of words, they have to introduce a symbol to stand for the unknown number themselves. By the end of the lesson the learners should understand everything in the Fact Box. Now would be a good time for the learners to make notes of these facts. Hopefully they will now think these facts obvious and feel more confident as mathematicians.

Using actions, images and algebra to model the mathematics

Think of a number n	☐	*The unknown number of counters in the box*
Add 2 $n + 2$	☐ ● ●	*Add 2 counters*
Multiply by 2 $2(n + 2) = 2n + 4$	☐ ☐ ● ● ● ●	*Double the boxes and double the counters*
Add 3 counters $2n + 7$	☐ ☐ ● ● ● ● ● ● ●	*Add 3 counters*
Subtract 5 $2n + 2$	☐ ☐ ● ●	*Remove 5 counters*
Now divide by 2 $n + 1$	☐ ●	*Take half the boxes and half the counters*
Subtract the number you first thought of	●	*Remove the box Leaving one counter*

In this problem, whatever the unknown number is the answer will always be 1!!

The crucial stages are shown in red: Multiply by 2 and later divide by 2.

These are inverse operations.

Dividing by 2 undoes the doubling of the boxes.

Once you have just one box left you take it away and everyone has the same number of counters.

This is just an interesting puzzle. It becomes mathematics when you start thinking about **why** it works. Then the idea of inverse operations becomes clearer.

Now try to invent a puzzle that always gives the same answer for yourself. Use the box below.

Think of a number n	☐	*The unknown number of counters in the box*
Add 1 $n + 1$	☐ ●	*Add 1 counter*
Multiply by 3 $3(n + 1) = 3n + 3$		*three boxes and three counters*
Add ... counters		*Add as many counters as you like*
Subtract ... counters		*Remove some counters* *Make sure you leave 3, 6 or 9 counters so it will be easy to divide by3*
Now divide by 3		*This leaves just one box and some counters*
Subtract the number you first thought of		*Remove the box and see how many counters you have left*

Key questions to develop understanding

- What is the inverse of adding five?
- What is the inverse of multiplying by four?
- What is the inverse of turning 90° clockwise?
- What is the inverse of taking two steps forward?

Helping learners remember

Making memorable mathematical notes

Encourage the learners to add colourful cartoon-like notes to help them remember the formal mathematical notes that you give them. They have found out in the four fours activity that you can use brackets to make an expression say exactly what you want:

(Bossy Brackets first)

Indices next up here look at me

Division and Multiplication ... last of all Addition and Subtraction

In a later grade you might want to use something like BODMAS to help learners remember the order of operations though it is not essential. O is an unhelpful letter standing for Order or Of. More useful is BIDMAS where I stands for Indices or BEDMAS if learners are more familiar with the word Exponents.

Whichever version you use it is not enough by itself to guide learners through all the pitfalls of evaluating complex expressions. They need to zoom in on the different parts of the expression. A teaching approach which can help is the idea of working on Fiendishly Difficult expressions. Instead of giving learners an exercise with simple problems leading slowly and rather boringly to more difficult problems, put one really difficult problem on the board and spend time – perhaps 10 or 15 minutes really getting the class involved in the problem. **Never** say this is easy, always emphasise how difficult the problem is going to be but that together you can solve it. Showboards are useful to get answers from the whole class. If you don't have them get the learners to hold up answers on paper.

$$\frac{2 \times 8 - (73 - 3^2)^{\frac{1}{2}}}{2 + \sqrt{36}}$$

It looks **horrible**! How to make sense of it? Where do you start?

Stories you read from left to right. 'Once upon a time' not 'Upon time a once'.

For mathematical expressions you ZOOM in. Bossy brackets first:

$$\frac{2 \times 8 - (73 - 3^2)^{\frac{1}{2}}}{2 + \sqrt{36}}$$

On your showboards.
$$(73 - 3^2) = 64 = 64$$

Write this answer in the expression and now ZOOM to indices

$$\frac{2 \times 8 - 64^{\frac{1}{2}}}{2 + \sqrt{36}}$$

Show on your boards and and write the answers in the expression

$$\frac{2 \times 8 - 8}{2 + 6}$$

Although there aren't any brackets in sight the convention is that you work out the top, work out the bottom and then divide. The long line works like an invisible bracket. So we have

$$\frac{16 - 8}{2 + 6} = \frac{8}{8} = 1$$

After all that work. The answer is 1!!   Now is the time to set an exercise for homework.

Sequences and patterns

Teaching strategy: Visual and practical learning styles

Curriculum content

Recognise, describe and represent patterns and relationships

Prior knowledge needed

Understand the use of a letter to stand for a variable.

Intended Learning Outcomes

At the end of this activity teachers and learners will:

- Know what an algebraic expression means
- Understand the difference between the variable and the constant in an expression
- Be able to construct patterns to represent algebraic expressions
- Be able to find a formula to represent a growing pattern
- Appreciate the value of giving meaning to an algebraic expression
- Have experienced a practical activity to support their understanding

---

Fact box

A variable can take different values in an algebraic expression. Letters are used to represent variables.

A coefficient is a number by which variables are multiplied. A coefficient acts on a variable.

A constant stays the same in an algebraic expression.

Example: $4n + 1$ n is a variable.   It takes different values.

              4 is a coefficient.   It tells you how many of n you have got.

              1 is a constant.   It does not change.

Resources for this workshop

Lots of small objects, you will need two different sorts of small objects, e.g. beans and buttons, or red and blue counters. Photocopies of worksheet on page 68.

Workshop Activities for Teachers

Activity 1: Making sequences with bean counters

> - Beans or similar counters (e.g. buttons, stones, seeds)
>
> *Small groups or pairs*   *1 hour*

1. One teacher in the group should arrange the counters into this sequence of patterns.

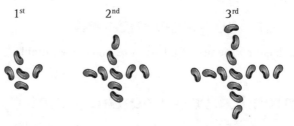

1st   2nd   3rd

   How many counters are there in each pattern?

   How is the pattern growing? Focus on the structure of the growing pattern.

   Another teacher should give precise instructions describing how to make the 8th pattern.

2. Can you predict the number of counters in the 4th pattern? 5th pattern? 10th pattern? 100th pattern?

3. Find an expression for the number of counters in the nth pattern in the sequence.

4. Work in pairs to create a sequence of patterns in which the nth pattern has $2n + 3$ counters. Discuss different series of patterns produced.

5. Go on to create sequence of patterns for more complex algebraic expressions.

Try this now

Notes

1. The pattern grows by adding four more counters – one on each 'arm' are added to the previous pattern with one counter in the middle. To make the 8th pattern put 8 counters on each of the 4 arms and one in the middle.

2. Numbers of counters: 4th pattern: 17; 5th pattern: 21; 10th pattern: 41; 100th pattern: 401.

3. $4n + 1$. Make sure you understand the relationship between the structure of the pattern and the algebraic expression. You could replace each middle counter in the patterns with another one of a different type or colour, to emphasise its position as the '+ 1'.

4. Try to find several different possible arrangements.

5. Focus on the structure of the patterns. Do some arrangements bring this out more clearly than others? For example, it is easier to see the growing 'arms'

   in this pattern:

   than in this one:

Activity 2: Bean counters and algebra

- Beans or similar counters (e.g. buttons, stones, seeds)

Pairs, whole group   *45 minutes*

1. Arrange counters into this sequence of patterns:

   1st   2nd   3rd

   Find an expression for the number of counters in the nth member of the sequence. Can you find more than one way of writing this expression?

   _____

2. Discuss how different ways of looking at the structure of the patterns can lead to different forms of algebraic expression.

   a

   $2n + 4$

   b

   $2(2 + n)$

                                                   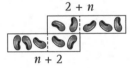

Try this now

3. Make a sequence of counters to show $4n + 4$. Can you see from your pattern that this is also $4(n + 1)$?

Notes

2. a $2n + 4$ will probably be the first suggestion.

   A constant 4 in the circle and two arms with n counters which grow longer and longer.

   b Looking at the pattern as two lines gives the formula $2(2 + n)$.

3. You can draw loops around the counters to show the two ways of looking at the arrangement, as above. Alternatively, use different counters to replace some parts of the pattern, one counter at a time. Be careful to show that you are not changing the pattern, just the items that you are using as counters.

   When $n = 3$ here are two ways of using different counters. The first diagram empasises 4 counters in the middle staying the same for the formula $2n + 4$.

   The second diagram emphasises two rows each with the same number ($n + 2$) of counters

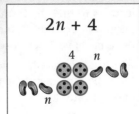

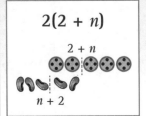

Classroom Activities for Learners

Activity 1: Counting beans

> • Two sorts of counter, e.g. beans and buttons, about 50 counters for each group
>
> *Pairs or small groups*   *50 minutes*

1. Draw the first series of patterns on the board   1ˢᵗ   2ⁿᵈ   3ʳᵈ

    Ask learners to copy the series with their own counters and to write down the number of counters in each pattern.

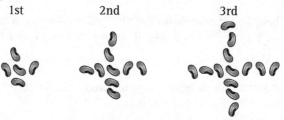

2. Ask how the pattern is growing. Focus on the structure of the growing pattern. Ask a learner to give precise instructions for drawing the 8th pattern.

3. Ask learners to predict the number of counters in the 4th pattern and 5th pattern.

4. Ask one or two learners to explain their reasoning.

5. Ask learners to predict the number of counters in the 10th and the 100th patterns.

6. Ask one or two learners to explain their reasoning.

7. Demonstrate the structure of the growing patterns by replacing the middle counters with an alternative, different one. Talk about the way that the 'arms' grow, but the counter in the middle is always there.

    Ask learners to replace the middle counters in their own patterns.

8. Introduce the expression $4n + 1$ for the number of counters in the nth pattern in the sequence.

9. Show learners a series of patterns in which the nth pattern has $2n + 3$ counters. Ask them to copy the patterns, then ask what the algebraic expression could be. Encourage them to see that $2n + 3$ and $3 + 2n$ are both correct. Again, emphasise the relationship between the structure of the patterns and the algebraic equation.

10. Ask learners to create a series of patterns for $3n + 4$. Compare different layouts of the patterns. Establish that they all have the same underlying structure.

11. Work on further series of patterns.

> **Teaching ideas**
>
> **1 & 2.** Notice how after looking at the 1st, 2nd and 3rd patterns there is a jump to ask about the 8th pattern. This jump is really important because you want the learners to find the **formula** for the sequence not just the next term. Learners need to notice that in the 2nd pattern the arms have 2 beans, in the 3rd pattern the arms have 3 beans so in the 8th pattern the arms will have 8 beans.
>
> **3 & 4.** The learners should have two ways of working these out: by adding 4 counters to the pattern each time and by knowing that in the 5th pattern each arm will have 5 beans so $4 \times 5 +$ one in the middle.
>
> **5 & 6** Adding 4 takes too long for the 100th but $4 \times 100 + 1$ will give you the answer.

Activity 2: Matching patterns to expressions

- Worksheet of patterns and expressions on page **68**
- Scissors

Pairs or small groups   *30 minutes*

Photocopy the worksheet on page **68** for the learners. The learners should cut out these expressions for the nth term and match them to the correct sequence on the worksheet.

$3n + 4$ $2n + 1$ n^2 $4n + 3$ $2n^2 - 1$ $2n + 1$

As the groups match the expressions to the patterns, ask them **why** they have chosen the expression for that pattern. Can they see the connection between the formula and the number of 'arms' to the pattern? Is there a connection with the number of shapes at the centre of the pattern?

Teaching ideas

- Ask learners who finish quickly to choose one of the patterns and:
  - Draw the next pattern in the sequence.
  - Work out how many counters in the 10th and the 100th pattern.
- You will find more questions to ask on page **67**.

Changes in my classroom practice

Implementing the teaching strategy

Visual and practical   *see page 4*

Concrete Representations

You can use small objects and diagrams to model a mathematical sequence. A sequence of patterns can offer a concrete, physical representation of the abstract algebraic expression. Visualising the patterns gives the learner a 'model to think with' which will support their understanding of what is happening when they manipulate algebraic expressions.

Many learners find it difficult to put any meaning into an abstract algebraic expression. They may learn some techniques for manipulating expressions and equations, but without a basic underlying understanding of what the variables and the numbers represent this may be quite meaningless. This may lead to errors as learners forget the 'rules' for manipulating algebra.

There is no one 'correct' representation of any particular expression. Different learners will come up with different patterns for the same expression. They should be encouraged to look at several patterns for each expression, and to discuss what is different and what is the same.

Changing the middle counter helps learners to visualise the pattern as 4 × arms plus 1. If you now ask for several large easy numbers 20th, 30th, 1000th then some learners may be able to say that for any number (nth) the number of beans is 4 times the number plus 1 or $4n + 1$.

Differentiation

Using practical apparatus can make it easier to differentiate the task. All learners can be asked to make the first few patterns for a sequence. Learners can choose to make simple patterns based on letters of the alphabet such as T or X or Y.

Learners who want a challenge could create patterns for expressions such as $2n^2 + 3n$.

It may be easier to start by building the third or fourth pattern in the series in order to see how they are structured, and then working backwards to the earlier patterns.

In the $n = 2$ pattern, can you spot the two 2×2 squares?

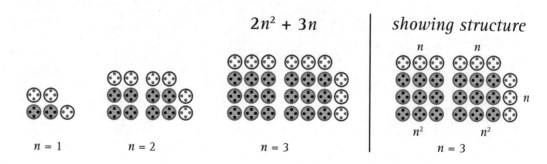

Key questions to develop understanding

You can ask the learners the following questions in relation to any sequence of patterns for which there is an algebraic expression for the nth term.

- Draw the next pattern in the sequence.
- Explain how to draw the next pattern in the sequence.
- How many extra objects would you use to change this pattern into the next pattern in the sequence?
- Tell me how many objects there are in each of the first four patterns in the sequence. Do those numbers follow a pattern?
- Could you tell me how many objects there are in the next pattern in the sequence without making or drawing the pattern? How did you work that out?
- How would you find out how many objects there are in the 10th pattern in the sequence?
- How would you find out how many objects there are in 100th pattern in the sequence?
- Can you find an algebraic expression (formula) for the number of objects in each pattern in the sequence?

Helping learners remember

Posters

Groups of learners could create posters showing how the structure of one sequence of patterns relates to the expression for the nth pattern in the sequence. Having some posters on the wall and talking about them occasionally will help to fix the ideas. Give the group squared paper and the triangle dotty paper (page 200) so they can draw several sequences. Each poster should have a question, e.g. How many triangles in the 10th shape?

Mental Mathematics

What is the value?

Write a formula in the middle of the board: $4 + 3n$.

Give the learners a number for n and ask them to work out the value of the expression. If you have showboards ask everyone to show you their answer and you will know immediately if they understand. If you don't have showboards the learners can write down their answers and mark each other's after you have given several values for *n*.

Quiet counting

Use the expression $4 + 3n$ and draw the first few patterns using counters. Ask the class to guess whether any of the patterns in the sequence will have exactly 100 counters. Show hands for yes, show hands for no. Encourage the learners just to make a guess – they won't be sure at this stage.

Now very quietly lead the class in counting 7, 10, 13, 16, 19, 23, ... and continue to see if you hit 100.

A few days later you can repeat with different numbers. These regular few minutes of mental maths at the beginning of the lesson can really help learners to remember ideas.

Match each sequence to the expression for the nth pattern in the sequence

Sequence A

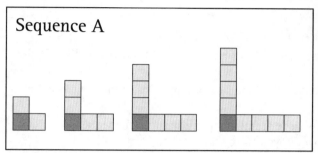

Sequence B

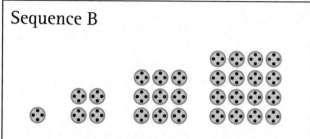

Sequence C

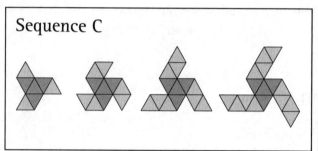

Sequence D

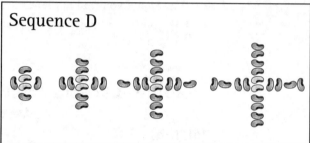

Sequence E

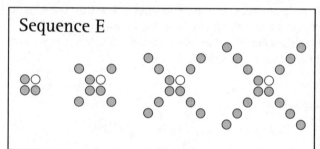

Sequence F

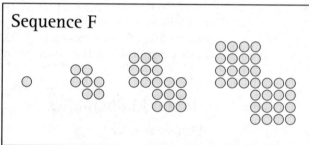

Expressions for the nth pattern. Cut out and match to the correct sequence

$3n + 4$	$2n + 1$	n^2
$4n + 3$	$2n^2 - 1$	$2n + 1$

Chapter 8

Functions and inverse functions

Teaching strategy: Visual and getting feedback

Curriculum content

Recognise, describe and represent patterns and relationships. Solve problems using algebraic language and skills.

Prior knowledge needed

Four operations with number, inverse of the four operations.

Intended Learning Outcomes

At the end of this activity teachers and learners will:

- Know how to recognise number patterns and describe them in words
- Understand how the description in words can be written using algebraic notation
- Be able to interpret simple algebraic expressions
- Appreciate patterns in numbers
- Have experienced a variety of activities using a visual learning style.

Fact box

A function is a calculation or set of calculations that can be carried out on an input number to produce an output number.

The inverse of a function is a calculation that sends the set of output numbers back to the input numbers.

The inverse of the function "Add 2" is "Subtract 2"

The inverse of the function "Multiply by 4" is "Divide by 4"

The function n goes to (n multiplied by 2) or $n \times 2$

is usually written as $n \longrightarrow 2n$

The inverse function is written as $n \longrightarrow \dfrac{n}{2}$

Resources for this workshop
Showboards, large sheet of paper or whiteboard; two differently coloured pens.

Workshop Activities for Teachers

Activity 1: Function game in silence

- Board and pens

Whole group   *45 minutes*

Choose someone to be the 'teacher' who will be at the board with the pen. Before beginning it is essential to emphasise that there is no talking and no discussion whilst the game is in progress. SILENCE IS IMPORTANT! If someone shouts out the pattern the activity is spoilt for everyone else.

Instructions for the 'teacher': Write the following on the board:

$$2 \longrightarrow 4$$
$$3 \longrightarrow 6$$
$$4 \longrightarrow$$

Hold up the pen and invite someone to come and write an answer. You now have to indicate whether the answer is correct or incorrect without speaking. If the number is wrong shake your head and rub it out.

Smile if the answer is correct.

$$2 \longrightarrow 4$$
$$3 \longrightarrow 6$$
$$4 \longrightarrow 8$$
$$5 \longrightarrow 10$$

After continuing in this way for other different starting numbers a pattern begins to develop. Usually work with consecutive numbers on the left-hand side until it is obvious from faces that most people understand.

Then start to make it a little more difficult by jumping to bigger numbers. At this stage you will become aware that some people are reading the vertical patterns in the table. So if 6 is written – they would write 12 but if 10 is written they would still write 12 because they are seeing the vertical addition of 2 on the right-hand side.

But some people will have recognised the rule that is being applied. At this point you need to focus on those people who have not yet spotted the pattern and build the pattern again.

Use numbers that make the rule obvious. So write:

$$20 \longrightarrow 40$$
$$30 \longrightarrow 60$$
$$40 \longrightarrow 80$$
$$50 \longrightarrow 100$$

Ask for the rule in words (speaking is allowed now). Likely responses are 'double the number' or 'multiply by 2'. Write   number $\longrightarrow$ number $\times 2$.

Hold out the pen again and invite someone to write something on the board taking n for the first number   so $n \longrightarrow n \times 2$ or $n \longrightarrow 2n$.

Now take turns to choose a function. Write it down without letting anyone else see. Take it in turns to give the lesson as above but using your own secret function. Continue giving examples until everyone in the group can guess the rule. Then ask for the rule to be written as $n \longrightarrow ?$

Activity 2: Extending the function game

* Large board; pens

Pairs, group   *45 minutes*

Functions that can be written in more than one way

The function 'double the number and add 2' can be written as

$$n \longrightarrow 2n + 2$$

When you play the function game some learners may spot the pattern as 'Add one to the number and double it'

$$n \longrightarrow (n + 1) \times 2$$

or $\quad n \longrightarrow 2(n + 1)$

This describes exactly the same function as

$$2n + 2 = 2(n + 1)$$

Everyone in the group should choose a secret function which can be written in more than one way and present it to the group in silence as described in Activity 1: Function game. Continue until there are lots of examples on the board and everyone is confident of the function before allowing anyone to speak. Then ask for the function to be described first in words and then as $n \longrightarrow ?$ The group should be able to find two different ways of describing the function.

Inverse functions

When you have finished a function game. Take a different coloured pen and draw arrows back from the final number to the starting number. These arrows show the inverse function.

2 4   8 16

30 60   ? 24

The function is 'double the number', which can be written $n \longrightarrow 2n$

The inverse function is 'divide the number by 2', which can be written

$$n \longrightarrow \frac{n}{2}$$

Everyone in the group takes the lead in being the teacher and introducing a function and then, by drawing arrows backwards, the inverse function.

Notes
* Experiment with slightly different ways of presenting the game. What happens if you choose random starting numbers instead of a sequence of numbers? Which numbers seem to be helpful in guessing? Try scattering the numbers around the board rather than lining them up in a column. Try including fractions or decimals.
* Lots of examples make it easier to guess the rule – around 20 may be needed.
* You may like to draw a smiley face on the board for a correct answer or hold up a showboard with a smiley face. 😊

Classroom Activities for Learners

Activity 1: Function game

- Large board

Whole class   *50 minutes*

What the teacher is doing

Explain to the class that they must be absolutely silent. Choose a function and write the first few examples on the board.

Continue the activity as described in Teacher Activity 1. Add lots of numbers. Try large starting numbers and possibly fractions.

Continue the game in silence until you think almost everyone has guessed the rule.

Tell the learners they are **now allowed to speak** and ask for the rule in words. Ask if anyone can write the rule more shortly using n for the starting number.

What the learners are doing

What the learners are doing

Learners watch the board. It should be very quiet and the learners should not put up their hands.

$$1 \longrightarrow 5$$
$$2 \longrightarrow 6$$
$$3 \longrightarrow 7$$
$$4 \longrightarrow 8$$
$$8 \longrightarrow \,?$$

The teacher walks around the class and offers the pen to a learner. The learner enters their guess for the number and hopes to get a smile.

After some time learners are allowed to speak. They may say:

You add on 4 each time *or*

number $\longrightarrow$ number plus 4 *or*

$n \longrightarrow n + 4$

Teaching ideas

- The initial objective is that learners will:
  - Recognise number patterns and represent them by a function.
  - Use letters to represent numbers.
- Play the game using all the ideas in Teacher Activity 1. You will need lots of practice with single step functions – that is additions, multiplications, subtractions and division, before going on to the two-step functions.
- The box shows a sample two-step function. Do you have enough information in the box to decide what the function is? You will often need around 20 examples on the board before everyone has guessed the function.

$$1 \longrightarrow 1 \qquad\qquad 20 \longrightarrow 39$$
$$2 \longrightarrow 3 \qquad\qquad 1000 \longrightarrow 1999$$
$$3 \longrightarrow 5$$
$$8 \longrightarrow 15$$

What is the rule?

You double the number and take away one

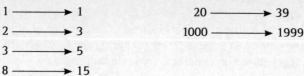

number $\longrightarrow$ number × 2   then take away 1

$n \longrightarrow 2n - 1$

Activity 2: Extending the function game

- Large board and pens

Whole class   *50 minutes*

What the teacher is doing	What the learners are doing
Functions that can be written in more than one way	
Choose a function that can be written in more than one way. Keep adding examples until you think everyone has guessed the rule.	Learners guess the function. Here are some examples:

$$5 \longrightarrow 18$$
$$6 \longrightarrow 21$$
$$7 \longrightarrow 24$$
$$8 \longrightarrow 27$$
$$10 \longrightarrow 33$$
$$20 \longrightarrow 63$$
$$100 \longrightarrow 303$$

What the teacher is doing	What the learners are doing
Explain that both expressions are correct.	Some learners may guess the rule as
$(n + 1) \times 3$ is usually written as $3(n + 1)$ and $3(n + 1)$ means exactly the same as $3n + 3$.	'three times the number plus 3' $$n \longrightarrow 3n + 3$$ or 'add one to the number and multiply by 3' $$n \longrightarrow (n + 1) \times 3$$
Inverse functions	
Play the function game with a one-step function, e.g. 'multiply by 3'.	Learners guess the function.
Leave all the examples on the board.	'number is multiplied by 3' $$n \longrightarrow 3n$$
Tell the class they must be silent again and concentrate. This time write the output number on the board and hand the pen to a learner to fill in the **input** number.	$$5 \quad 15 \qquad ? \quad 30$$ Learners know the function is multiply by 3 but now it is not the output number they have to guess but the input number.
After a while ask for the inverse function.	Learners describe the inverse function, first in words.
Repeat for other functions.	Divide by 3.
	Then as $$n \longrightarrow n \div 3$$
	Or $$n \longrightarrow \frac{n}{3}$$

Teaching ideas

- Don't tell the learners that there is more than one way to describe the rule just ask if anyone has a different way of describing the rule. If you get two different formulae, ask the class which one they think is correct. Get them to explain to you that both are correct! It greatly boosts the confidence of a learner if they are doing the explaining rather than the teacher.

- Drawing another arrow in a different colour back from the output to a question mark for the input emphasises that the inverse function takes you back to where you started.

Changes in my classroom practice

Implementing the teaching strategy

Visual learning   see page 4
Getting feedback   see page 10

Visual learning

What is the point of the silence? This is a learning device. All pupils come to an understanding of the rule at different stages. Calling out the rule spoils that moment at which the child realises that they understand. The pupils are starting from a problem not a technique. The silence helps you to read faces and it is very clear when they understand so this enables you to **find out what learners understand**. Because there is no auditory input the learners must concentrate on the **visual**.

Kinaesthetic learning

The silence makes it dramatic as an individual learner comes to the board and writes. As you walk around the class and offer the pen you will learn to judge when learners are ready to write on the board. You can stage-manage the situation so that confident learners are given the pen for a complicated number and less confident learners for simpler ones.

Adapting the activity for a large class

If your class is large you can involve more learners by using showboards. Explain at the beginning that they must be silent and that when you point to the whiteboard they must write on their showboards the number they think goes at the end of the arrow. Point to someone with the correct answer to come and write it on the board or get them to pass their board forward if movement is difficult. You can then show the board to the class and write the number on the large whiteboard yourself. You will not need to rub out any answers as you can always choose someone with the correct answer. You will also have a very good idea of how many learners have guessed the pattern.

Key questions to develop understanding

This is a silent activity so the teacher uses few questions! Instead of spoken questions the teacher writes on the board and offers the pen. The crucial questions at the end of the activity are:

- What is the rule?
- Can you write it differently?
- Can you write the rule more shortly by using n to stand for the number?

Follow up activity

One and two stage inverse functions

Once the learners are confident that

- addition and subtraction are inverse operations
- multiplication and division are inverse operations

You can work on the inverse of two stage functions. If the learners are good at guessing functions then they should be able to guess that

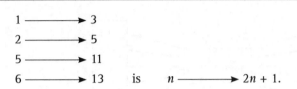

$$1 \longrightarrow 3$$
$$2 \longrightarrow 5$$
$$5 \longrightarrow 11$$
$$6 \longrightarrow 13 \qquad \text{is} \qquad n \longrightarrow 2n + 1.$$

Now try that backwards

$$3 \longrightarrow 1$$
$$5 \longrightarrow 2$$
$$11 \longrightarrow 5$$
$$13 \longrightarrow 6$$

Dividing by 2 seems an obvious idea – but that gives fractions.

Taking away one first and then dividing by two is what you need $\quad n \longrightarrow \dfrac{(n-1)}{2}$

We all know that the inverse of 'putting on your socks and your shoes' is **not** 'taking off your socks and then taking off your shoes'.

Flow diagrams work well to demonstrate this.

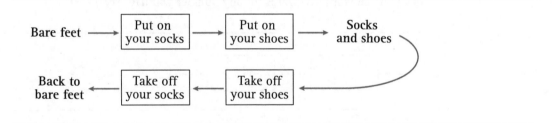

Get the learners to think of more examples. For example:

- put on your school uniform – go to school – come home from school – take off your uniform.
- go to the moon – land on the moon – take off from the moon – come back to earth.

As long as both actions have an inverse this will work.

- stand up – leave the room – come back in the room – sit down

It is like running a film backwards: you undo the last thing you did so

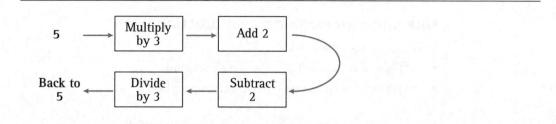

Use the idea of inverse operations to find the missing numbers:

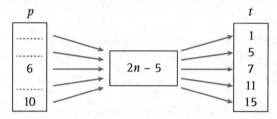

To solve this problem first try running the film forward using number 6 which the function $2n - 5$ sends to 7

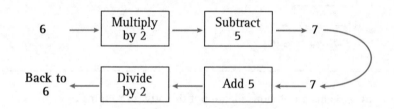

Then run the film backwards the inverse of subtract 5 is add 5 and inverse of multiply by 2 is divide by 2.

Now you can work backwards for any number you like. Try 1

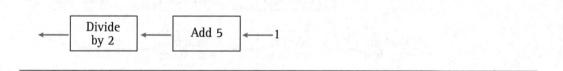

Developing algebraic skills

Teaching strategy: Starting from a problem not a technique

Curriculum content

Understand, manipulate and substitute in algebraic expressions; begin to set up and solve linear equations

Prior knowledge needed

Some understanding of simple expressions and equivalent forms of expressions; some experience of substituting numbers in simple expressions (but these will all be developed during the activity)

Intended Learning Outcomes

At the end of this activity teachers and learners will:

- Know how to use algebra to solve puzzles
- Understand that an equation is a 'clue' to a number
- Be able to manipulate linear expressions
- Appreciate that algebra is a generalised form of number
- Have experienced ways of using algebra to solve simple problems

Fact box

Useful techniques used in the puzzles in this chapter:

Addition and subtraction of integers, fractions and decimals

Using algebraic expressions to explain a pattern in numbers

Addition and subtraction of algebraic expressions
e.g. $3a + 8 - (2a + 3) = a + 5$

Evaluating algebraic expressions when the value of the variables is known
e.g. evaluate $2a + 3b$ when $a = -2$ and $b = 4$

Solving simple linear equations

Resources for this workshop
Pencil and paper; photocopy of worksheets on pages 83 and 84.

Workshop Activities for Teachers

Activity 1: A number puzzle

> • Pencil and paper
>
> *Pairs or groups of 3*   *50 minutes*

Solving and inventing problems

In a number pyramid, each box is the sum of the 2 boxes it rests on. Can you fill in the gaps?

Now try the worksheet on page **83**.

Notice that this worksheet is not just a list of questions. You are given one or two examples and then asked to **invent** problems for yourself. Inventing problems is the important part and you should spend most of your time on this.

Is there any restriction on the sort of numbers you could use? Invent a pyramid that uses fractions or decimals?

Each pair should choose one of these questions. When you have worked on your question explain your findings to the whole group and answer their questions.

- How can you "work backwards" to find numbers on the bottom row?
- Does it matter which boxes you are given?
- Is there always only one answer? How do you know?
- How can you predict the box at the top if you are given the bottom row?

- What is the same, and what is different, if you use algebra rather than numbers?

Presentations

Now that you have a good understanding of the puzzle choose someone to act as teacher and present the puzzle as you would to your class using just the first two examples from the worksheet. Discuss how well your teacher succeeded in:

- Getting the group involved in solving and inventing puzzles.
- Making the transition from numbers to algebra seem natural.

> **Notes**
> Presenting the problem to the whole class without a worksheet can work well as you can encourage them to invent more and more puzzles for themselves. Showboards are helpful in getting feedback.

Activity 2: Another number puzzle

- Pencil and paper

Pairs of groups of 3   *40 minutes*

Each square is the sum of the numbers in the 2 circles next to it. Can you fill in the missing numbers?

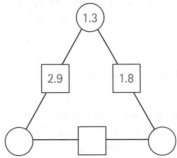

Try this now

Try the worksheet on page **84**.

Each pair should choose one of these questions to work on:

- How do you find the numbers in the squares? So how do you find the numbers in the circles?
- Does your answer work? Is it the only answer? How do you know?
- What could you change to make this easier for your learners? How could you make it harder?

Work on your question and then present your findings to the group.

Notes

At first this seems like a simple number puzzle, something you might spend a few minutes on and then move on. If you take the time to try some triangle puzzles and invent some of your own you will find that it is a useful tool which you can use to help your learners:

- Become more confident at tackling problems.
- Practice numerical and algebraic techniques
- Check their own answers.

Here is an example of how the triangles provide practice with equations and negative numbers, including substitution. Put any numbers you like in the boxes. Try a few guesses – if you can't find the solution put an x in the top circle.

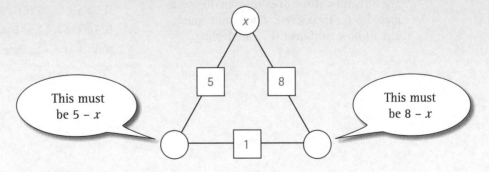

So from the bottom line of the pyramid we know $(5 - x) + (8 - x) = 1$

Solving this equation to get $x = 6$ gives useful **practice with a negative coefficient for x.**

To see if our answer is correct we need to substitute. $5 - x = 5 - 6 = -1$ and $8 - x = 8 - 6 = 2$

Are we correct? $-1 + 2 = 1$ Yes that is the answer in the box.

Classroom Activities for Learners

Activity 1: A number puzzle
(based on Number Pyramids worksheet)

- Showboards
- At least one copy of the Number Pyramids worksheet page 83

Whole class and pairs   *40 minutes*

Ideas for teaching

This activity may be worked on in groups using copies of the worksheet or the worksheet on a board; or the *ideas* may be used to structure whole-class teaching, using 'show-me' boards to give answers so everyone has to take part.

First introduce number pyramids with bottom row given, then different boxes given. When learners have written some of their own and tested them on each other, move to using algebra – first one variable, then two for more confident learners. *Always* expect learners to check that their solutions work, and when they find solutions in algebra, to see what they look like for a particular value of the variable: does the pyramid still work? If they are making up their own pyramids using algebra, suggest they use the first letter of their name as a variable – it gives them 'ownership'.

Only take learners as far as they can go with reasonable effort: it's better that they make up lots of their own at a level they are happy with, and build up their confidence. You can return to do more, and perhaps harder, later. The difficulty of the ones they are happy to make up for themselves gives you a good idea of how confident they are feeling.

Solutions to worksheet:

1. **a)** 20 at top
    b) 14, 1 in bottom row

    Top number $= a + 2b + c$ if the bottom row is a, b, c: accept any words which explain this, and perhaps encourage learners to give examples, and then to express it in algebra.

2. **a)** $4a + 4$
    b) $a + 2$

3. **a)** $2a + 5b + 6$ (Can learners make the link with their answer to question 1? If not, support them in doing so.)

4

5. If $4a + 4 = 24$ then $a = 5$ so the pyramid is:

    ```
        24
      12  12
     5   7   5
    ```

    If $3a + 8 = 29$ then $a = 7$
    If $3a + 8 = 12.5$ then $a = 1.5$
    If $3a + 8 = -22$ then $a = -10$

Activity 2: Another number puzzle
(based on Triangle Puzzles worksheet)

- Showboards; paper and pencils
- At least one copy of the triangle puzzles worksheet page 84

Whole class or group work   *30 minutes*

Ideas for teaching

This activity may be done in groups using the worksheet (either by making copies of the worksheet or by writing it on the board); or the *ideas* may be used to structure whole-class teaching, using showboards to give answers so everyone has to take part. A different structure from that used for Number Pyramids gives variety. This activity could be used in the lesson after Number Pyramids, or at a later stage.

First introduce the idea of adding the numbers in the circle to get the number in the square. When learners show they can follow the idea with easy numbers in all circles they are ready to try harder versions. As above, the more learners do for themselves in pairs or small groups the more confident they will be, especially if they can make up their own questions.

At a later stage, learners could try puzzles with harder algebraic expressions – or to practise fractions, decimals or negative numbers.

Solutions to worksheet:

1. a) 13
    b) 8
    c) 7
    d) 11, 12, 15
    e) 36, 42, 40
    f) $2x + 1$, $3x + 3$, $3x + 4$
    g) 4, 7, 7
    h) 1.6, 2.1, 0.5
    i) $2x$, $3x + y$, $x + y$
2. a) 5, 3, 4
    b) 7, 6, 0
    c) 1.3, 1.2, 2.8

Learners may be able to 'spot' answers in easy cases, but for example in part a if the top number is x then the 2 bottom numbers are $8 - x$ and $9 - x$, so $8 - x + 9 - x = 7$.

Changes in my classroom practice

Implementing the teaching strategies

Starting from a problem not a technique   *see page 12*

It is possible for learners to master techniques by doing lots of exercises. An alternative approach is to give the learner a problem or puzzle which they can only solve by using the techniques you want them to practice. So the learners will be mastering the technique and also doing some mathematical thinking. This is usually much more interesting than an exercise so the learners will be more involved and work harder.

Once the idea of **number pyramids** is understood, they can be used to practise number work of any sort, as well as a variety of algebra, so once the idea is familiar they can be used again. More layers can be added if needed. They are easy to check, and to differentiate, and learners enjoy making up their own for friends. Working in pairs or a small group helps clarify ideas and give confidence.

The **triangle puzzles** are also versatile, and can be used in different shapes, e.g. squares, but 'working backwards' is probably harder.

If learners are encouraged to find solutions to algebraic problems and then check using any value for the variable(s), they will begin to appreciate the power of algebra to represent general situations: that will be particularly clear if they then have the opportunity to work with the magic square reference given below.

Key questions to develop understanding

Puzzle 1

- How can you 'work backwards' to find numbers on the bottom row?
- Does it matter which boxes you are given? Is there only one answer? How do you know?
- How can you predict the box at the top if you are given the bottom row?
- What is the same, and what is different, if you use algebra rather than numbers?

If a learner asks "Is this right?" reply "Does it work?" so that they are relying on themselves and not the teacher.

Puzzle 2

- How do you find the numbers in the squares?
- So how do you find the numbers in the circles?
- Does your answer work? Is it the only answer? How do you know?

Follow up activities

Triangle puzzle

http://nrich.maths.org/2670 has an interactive version of the triangle puzzle called arithmagons where learners (or teachers!) can make the puzzle as hard as they choose.

Magic Sums and products

http://nrich.maths.org/1376 shows you how to make as many magic squares as you like, by substituting in an algebraic magic square: try it! (Magic squares have both diagonals and every row and column with the same total, which has to be 3 times the middle number – why?) Can your class make a different magic square each?

Number Pyramids

(Questions with a * are harder)

1. In a number pyramid each number is the sum of the numbers in the 2 boxes below it. Can you complete these two?

a)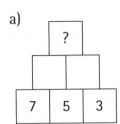

b)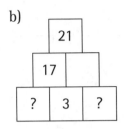

In pairs, make up one for each other to try. Can you find a way of predicting what the top number is going to be if you are given the bottom 3 numbers?

2. We can use number pyramids with algebra also. What do you think the missing box should be in these two pyramids? In each case, make up a similar one of your own and ask a friend to try it. You might like to use the first letter of your own name instead of '*a*'.

a)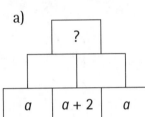

b)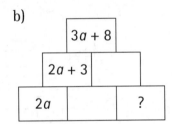

3* What about these? They are more difficult, so are for learners who think question 2 is too easy!

a)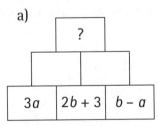

b)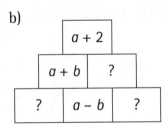

4. If we know what a letter is worth, we can turn a number pyramid made of algebra into one made of numbers. Re-draw the pyramid in question **2b** for when a is worth **7**. Does it still work? Now choose your own number instead of **7**. (It doesn't have to be a whole number!)

5* Sometimes we have a clue to what a number is worth. In question **2a**, if the top box is worth 24, can you work out what the pyramid must look like in numbers? In question **2b**, what if the top box is worth 29? 12.5? –22? Can you make up your own similar questions?

Triangle Puzzles

(Questions with a * are harder)

1. In these puzzles the number in a square is the sum of the numbers in the 2 circles next to it. Can you complete these? 'x' and 'y' could be any numbers – try it and see!

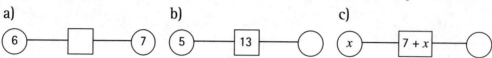

a) b) c)

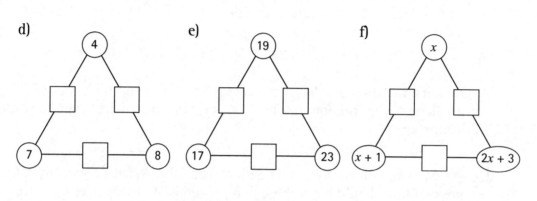

d) e) f)

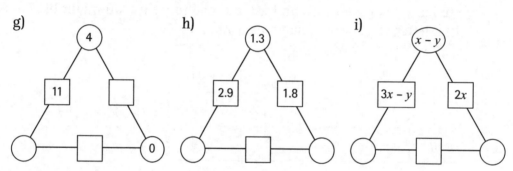

g) h) i)

2* These ones are harder, so it might be easier to work in pairs or in a group. If you get stuck, you might want to call one of the numbers in a circle 'x' and see if you can work out what the other numbers have to be from that. If you can find all the missing numbers, try making up some for the rest of your group. You can use any sort of numbers, positive or negative, or algebra.

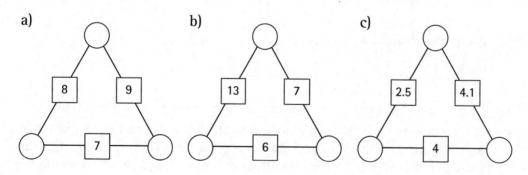

a) b) c)

Word problems and linear equations

Teaching strategy: Discussion

Curriculum content

Word problems leading to equations. Construct and solve linear equations

Prior knowledge needed

Using a letter to represent an unknown number. Construction and meaning of simple expressions.

Intended Learning Outcomes

At the end of this activity teachers and learners will:

- Know the difference between an expression and an equation
- Understand how to construct an equation from a simple relationship
- Understand how an equation can be manipulated to reach a solution
- Be able to solve simple equations and understand the meaning of the solution
- Appreciate the value of representing some situations algebraically
- Have experienced activities that link real problems with algebraic solutions

Fact box

An expression cannot tell us the value of an unknown number, it can only tell us its relationship with another unknown number.

An equation can tell us the value of an expression, so we can find the value of an unknown number.

The equals sign in an equation means the value of both sides is the same. So any mathematical operation that you do to one side, must also be done to the other to keep the value balanced. We can use this to manipulate equations to find the value of the unknown number.

Identifying what we need to find:
Doreen has 3 boxes of sweets and 7 extra sweets.

She has 43 sweets altogether.

What we don't know is how many sweets are in a box. Call this unknown value y.

Then $3y + 7$ is an expression describing 3 whole boxes of sweets and 7 extra sweets.

We know there are 43 sweets altogether.

Now the word problem can be written as an equation:

$$3y + 7 = 43.$$

Solving the equation gives us the number of sweets in a box.

Resources for teacher workshop
One photocopy per pair of the 'Stories and equations' sheet on page 92; scissors; few sheets of A4 paper.

Workshop Activities for Teachers

Activity 1: Matching stories and equations

- One photocopy per pair of the 'Stories and equations' sheet on page **92**;
- Scissors

Pairs   *30 minutes*

Cut out and shuffle the cards.

Place all the cards face down on the table. Take it in turns to turn over any two cards. If the pair of cards turned over are a matching story and equation, you win the pair. If not, turn them back face down.

When all the pairs have been matched both look at each pair in turn. Try to say what the letter in each equation stands for and work out its value.

Each person scores:

     1 point for each pair they match;

     1 point for each letter they correctly identify;

     1 point for each value of a letter they find out.

The winner is the person who scores most points.

Extension: Make up some more stories and matching equations to add to the game. Keep the stories simple and try to vary the equations that they match with.

> **Notes**
>
> To match the cards, look for similar numbers in the problem and in the equation and look for the relationship between the unknown letter and the numbers.
>
> The answers are:
>
> 1. x = no. of apples B has, $x = 6$;
>
> 2. y = no. of sweets in a box, $y = 12$;
>
> 3. n = original number of cows in the field, $n = 8$;
>
> 4. p = weight of one pencil, $p = 7$;
>
> 5. d = the number thought of, $d = 9$;
>
> 6. w = weight of one orange, $w = 40$;
>
> 7. b = no. of books P had to start with, $b = 12$;
>
> 8. m = the number I thought of, $m =$
>
>

Activity 2: From symbols to words and back again

- Paper; pencils/pens

Pairs or threes

45 minutes

1. **n + 3** What does this mean? What situations could it describe?

   Make up some more examples of expressions. In each expression, what does the unknown number represent?

2. Think of some situations described by these expressions:

   $a + 100$ $2m$ $p - 5$ $2x + 3$

3. The expression $a + 100$ can be made into an equation, e.g. $a + 100 = 103$ and then we can say what the value of a is, namely $a = 3$. Make some of your expressions into equations and say what the value of the unknown number is and what this value represents.

4. Write $p = 3$ in the middle of the page. Around it write other equations which also have the value 3 for p. Write as many different equations as you can. Discuss how you made each one. What mathematical operations did you use?

Notes

1 & 2. For example: 'I was on a bus and three more people got on'; n means the number of people on the bus before three more got on, or 'John has three more cows than George'; n means the number of cows George has.

3. For example: $n + 3 = 27$: 'An apple costs 27 cents today. This is 3 cents more than last week. $n = 24$, so last week an apples cost 24 cents. n is the cost of the apple last week.'

4. Can you see how each of these has been formed? They use mathematical operations such as add 2, subtract 1, multiply by 10, multiply by 2, multiply by 3 and add 1. The operations are used on **both** sides of the equation.

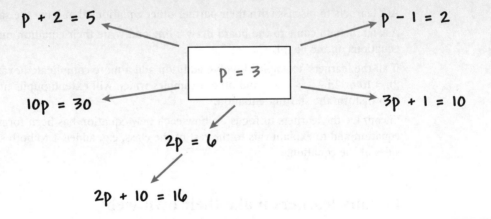

Classroom Activities for Learners

Activity 1: Matching stories and equations

- Photocopy the stories and equations sheet on page **92**.

Pairs   *50 minutes*

In pairs learners discuss equations

Organise the class in pairs each with a copy of the stories and equations sheet. Learners should first cut out and shuffle the cards. Explain how to play the game described in the teachers' workshop. If you wrote any more pairs during the workshop, include these too.

> **Teaching ideas**
>
> Encourage learners to check and share their answers, explaining *why* each equation matches the word problem.

Activity 2: Making equations

- Paper and pens for making posters

Whole class and pairs   *50 minutes*

Class makes a web of equations on the board

Write $n = 5$ in the middle of the board. Then draw an arrow and write $n + 1 = 6$

Tell learners these equations are called 'equivalent' as they have the same value for n.

Ask learners to discuss with their partner other equations that have the same value for n.

Ask learners to come to the board draw a line and write their equation until there is a web of equations on the board.

If all the learners' examples involve addition add a more complicated example yourself, e.g. $2n = 10$ or $2n - 1 = n + 4$ and other examples which will extend pupils understanding of how to transform the starting equation.

Encourage the learners to focus on how each new equation has been formed from a previous equation and to explain this to the rest of the class, e.g. added 1 to both sides, doubled both sides of the equation.

In pairs learners make their own web

When a wide variety of equations has been added to the board and learners have explained how they are formed, ask each pair of learners to construct a 'web' of equations from a new starting equation. Leave the web generated by the class on the board to give learners support in developing their own. These webs could be made into posters for display.

> **Teaching ideas**
> - Emphasise that the equation is being changed by doing the **same operation** to both sides.
> - You need to judge when it is appropriate to introduce a new type of operation, for example with multiples of the unknown (e.g. $2n = 10$), or with the unknown appearing on both sides of the equation (e.g. $2n + 1 = n + 6$)
> - It is important to introduce new types of equation slowly and give all learners an opportunity to think about and express their understanding of how they are formed. Learners should be encouraged to discuss their ideas with others and any confusion should be explored with the whole class.
> - Encourage learners to use different letters as their unknown number when they make their own webs. For example, some can use x, some p, perhaps the first letter of their own name. This encourages them to be flexible in recognising that many letters can be used, not just x or n.

Activity 3: Solving equations

Whole class, pairs   *30 minutes*

Class solves equations

Explain that since all the equations in the last activity have the same value for the unknown number, we can choose suitable operations to help us find the value of the number.

Ask learners to discuss in pairs:

What operation can we do to both sides of $n + 7 = 10$ so that it only has n on the left side?

Ask each pair to write their answer on a showboard so that you get responses from the whole class. Give more examples of this type, e.g. $n + 6 = 8$, $n - 2 = 5$.

When learners seem confident ask:

What operation can we do to $4n = 14$ so that it only has n on the left side?

Give several examples of each type before moving on to equations that need two operations, e.g. $2n - 3 = 5$

Working in pairs to solve equations

Ask each learner to write down a simple equation then work in pairs to solve both their equations. Remind the learners to decide which operations to use to solve their equations. Encourage them to start with quite simple examples and then gradually increase the difficulty.

> **Teaching ideas**
> - It is important to note that a range of possible answers may all be mathematically correct but not necessarily useful. Learners need to gradually explore which are 'useful' operations and which are not. For example, it is not very useful to use '$-3n$' on the equation $4n = 14$ as $n = 14 - 3n$ does not help us find what n is worth. But the suggestion of '$-3n$' is not wrong!
> - Answers will not always be whole numbers – include examples with fractional and/or negative answers.
> - For $2n - 3 = 5$, if learners suggest '$\div 2$' before '$+3$' show how this still works: the equation becomes $n - 1\frac{1}{2} = 2\frac{1}{2}$ so the second operation is then '$+1\frac{1}{2}$'. Help learners to explore why both of these work and why it is usually easier to do $+/-$ operations before $\times / \div$ operations.

Changes in my classroom practice

Implementing the teaching strategy

Discussion	*see page 8*

It is very helpful to share ideas about algebra and talk about what you understand. Encourage learners to discuss what they understand, so that confusion can be expressed and dealt with. These ideas can feel quite abstract to learners, so links to real contexts can help – but be careful not to limit possibilities in this way. For example, it is important for learners to experience negative and fractional answers to equations and not only positive whole numbers.

In the matching game the learners need to study the statements carefully to see if they match. Learners who would be silent if asked directly to discuss a mathematical issue can often be heard discussing mathematical issues heatedly in the context of a game.

An important focus of the activities is how relationships are represented in algebraic notation. Discussion is important to help clarify this. In this case the letters represent unknowns – they each have a value that can be found by solving the equations.

These activities give learners the opportunity to construct their own equations and to explore collections of equations that have the same solution. In doing the activities and discussing them the learners gain a better insight into the concept of a variable and into algebraic processes.

Sometimes a weighing scales model is used to think about equations, with the two sides of the scales balanced. Discuss with your partner whether you think this would help learners and what problems it might present.

Key questions to develop understanding

- Can you explain what your letters stand for?
- Can you explain the equation in words?
- Can you spot what is the same in the words and in the equation?
- How has $n = 5$ been changed into $n + 1 = 6$? What mathematical operation has been done to both sides of the equation?

Follow up activity

Putting statements in order

1. Here is a sequence of equations but they are all jumbled up. Re-arrange the equations to show how to solve an equation. The last line will be the solution $a = 8$.

$$3a - 7 = 17$$
$$5a - 2a - 7 = 17 + 2a - 2a$$
$$a = 8$$
$$5a - 7 = 17 + 2a$$
$$3a = 24$$

2. Create a sequence of equations starting from a 'complex' one, ending with a 'simple' one, to find the value of an unknown number. Write each equation on a separate piece of paper and give it to another group. They must try to put the equations in order so that they can see the sequence of operations needed to find the value of the unknown number.

Solution to problem a

$5a - 7 = 17 + 2a$	(first $-2a$)
$5a - 2a - 7 = 17 + 2a - 2a$	(then simplify)
$3a - 7 = 17$	(then $+7$)
$3a = 24$	(then $\div 3$)
$a = 8$	

Success – in the last line you have found the value of a!

This activity is helpful for getting learners to **talk** about the mathematics.

Teachers working on the matching stories and equations activity

Matching stories and equations: Cut out these 16 cards and shuffle

1. A has 3 more apples than B. There are 15 apples all together.	$2x + 3 = 15$
2. Doreen has 3 whole boxes of sweets and 7 extra sweets. She has 43 sweets altogether	$3y + 7 = 43$
3. There were some cows in a field. 16 more cows came into the field. Now there are 3 times as many as there were before	$n + 16 = 3n$
4. 12 pencils weigh 84 gm	$12p = 84$
5. I think of a number, multiply it by 25 and add 30. The answer is 255.	$25d + 30 = 255$
6. 3 oranges weigh 120 g.	$3w = 120$
7. Phumi has some books. He is given 12 more. Now he has 3 times as many as before	$b + 12 = 3b$
8. I think of a number, multiply it by 5 and add 2. The answer is 47.	$5m + 2 = 47$

Working with brackets

Teaching strategy: Getting feedback

Curriculum content

Multiplying brackets by a single term and by other brackets; the difference of two squares and its use in mental arithmetic.

Prior knowledge needed

The use of variables and exponents.

Intended Learning Outcomes

At the end of this activity teachers and learners will:

* Know how to multiply brackets containing algebraic expressions together
* Understand the use of diagrams to explain algebraic procedures
* Be able to multiply out brackets accurately
* Appreciate how to use this to assist mental calculations
* Have experienced success learning how to do this

Fact box

Using a single bracket $\quad a(x + b) = ax + ab$

  e.g. $\qquad\qquad\qquad\quad 3(x - 5) = 3x - 15$

Multiplying two brackets $\quad (x + a)(x + b) = x^2 + ax + bx + ab$

  e.g. $\qquad\qquad\quad (x + 2)(x - 3) = x^2 + 2x - 3x - 6$

$\qquad\qquad\qquad\qquad\qquad\quad = x^2 \qquad\quad - x \qquad - 6$

(Notice how in this case the middle terms combine.)

A special case when $b = -a$ $\qquad (x + a)(x - a) = x^2 - a^2$

This is called the difference of squares.

$\qquad (x + 3)(x - 3) = x^2 + 3x - 3x - 9$

$\qquad\qquad\qquad = \qquad\quad x^2 \qquad - 9$

(Notice that in this case the middle terms cancel out.)

Resources for this workshop
Showboards or sheets of paper.

Workshop Activities for Teachers

Activity 1: Teaching algebraic techniques – use of brackets

> - Showboards
>
> *Whole group and pairs*   *1 hour*

Trying the classroom activities

Classroom Activities 1 and 2 show two approaches to working with brackets. Instead of starting with algebraic rules, Classroom Activity 1 starts with people maths and visualising areas. Activity 2 starts with a number activity. Once the learners understand how the number grids work, algebra is introduced. Choose two people to act as teachers and present Classroom Activities 1 and 2 to the group. The chosen teachers will have done a really good job if:

- they make clear to the rest of the group **what** they should be doing
- they try **not** to talk too much themselves but encourage the group to get involved
- they get the group to use their showboards.

Discussion

Do you prefer the area approach or the grid approach? What other approaches do you know? Which is simplest to understand?

Which is best for brackets with all positive numbers?

Which extends easily to brackets with negative numbers?

> **Notes**
>
> *Area method*
>
> Area diagrams are effective when considering positive terms. Using numbers gives a starting activity that all learners can understand. You can then gradually introduce variables. When drawing an area diagram you can choose any length for x as you don't know its value. Make the other lengths like 2 and 3 look about right.
>
> | | x | 3 |
> |-------|---------|-------|
> | x | x^2 | $3x$ |
> | 2 | $2x$ | 6 |
>
> Total area $= (x + 2)(x + 3)$
> Sum of area of small rectangles
> $$= x^2 + 2x + 3x + 6$$
> $$= x^2 + 5x + 6$$
>
> *Grid method*
>
> The grid method can be used for positive and negative terms
>
> | × | x | 2 |
> |-----|-------|------|
> | x | x^2 | $2x$ |
> | 3 | $3x$ | 6 |
>
> | × | x | −2 |
> |-----|-------|-------|
> | x | x^2 | $-2x$ |
> | 3 | $3x$ | −6 |
>
> | × | x | −2 |
> |-----|-------|-------|
> | x | x^2 | $-2x$ |
> | −3 | $-3x$ | $+6x$ |
>
> Notice which terms in the grid give the first and last terms of the expansion.
>
> Use colour or circling to emphasise the terms which combine to give the middle term, e.g. $(x + 3)(x - 2) = x^2 - 2x + 3x + 6 = x^2 + x + 6$

Formal methods

Learners may like to continue to use the area or grid methods or to move to more formal methods.

They should now understand why these methods work.

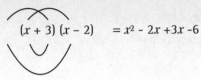

$$(x + 3)(x - 2) = x^2 - 2x + 3x - 6$$

Can you see the smiling face with mouth and eyebrows?

Activity 2: Using the difference of two squares for mental arithmetic

- Showboards or paper to hold up

Pairs   *30 minutes*

Work in pairs initially and then discuss as a group.

1. Work out: $2^2 - 1^2 =$, $3^2 - 2^2 =$, $5^2 - 4^2 =$, $8^2 - 7^2 =$
   What do you notice when you look at all the answers?
   Can you work out $19^2 - 18^2$ from the pattern?

2. Write $(x + a)(x - a)$ without brackets. Can you see how this helps to explain what you noticed in 1?

3. What is 30^2? That is quite easy, it is 900.
   But what is 31^2?

4. Write down 41^2, 61^2, 29^2, 101^2. (Use calculators only to check your answer.)

5. What is 31×29? 32×28? 33×27?
   Can you see the pattern? Can you work out 34×26 without a calculator?

Notes
1. In each case the answer is the sum of the numbers being squared, e.g. $5^2 - 4^2 = 9$.

   This activity shows how to use the expansion of brackets to explain this surprising result and how to use it to work out complicated square numbers in your head. Amaze your learners!

2. $x^2 - a^2 = (x + a)(x - a)$. When $x - a = 1$, $x^2 - a^2 = x + a$

   So for any pair of consecutive whole numbers the difference in their squares is their sum.

3. Answer $31^2 - 30^2 = (31 - 30)(31 + 30) = 61.$ So $31^2 = 30^2 + 61 = 961.$

4. This can be used for finding the squares of many numbers: What is 39^2?

   40^2 you can work out in your head. $40^2 - 39^2 = 79$ Rearrange to find $39^2 = 1600 - 79$

5. This extends the pattern to a difference of 2 or 3.

   $(30 + 2)(30 - 2) = 30^2 + 60 - 60 - 4 = 30^2 - 4$

Classroom Activities for Learners

Activity 1: Multiplying out brackets – using area

- Showboards

Whole class activity   *50 minutes*

People maths

Ask 12 boys and 8 girls to stand up and form 4 by 3 and 4 by 2 rectangles respectively

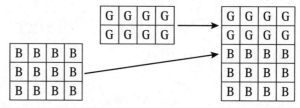

and then move together to make one big rectangle.

Show me on your boards:

- How many girls in the 4 × 2 rectangle?
- How many boys in the 4 × 3 rectangle?

 Now look at the whole rectangle of girls and boys.

› Write down the size of the rectangle and the total number of learners.

$$4 \times (2 + 3) = 4 \times 2 + 4 \times 3 = 20$$

Area method

Ask the learners to draw a rectangle measuring $(2 + 3)$ cm by $(4 + 5)$ cm. Try to work out the area in more than one way.

On your boards show how you worked it out.

Choose several learners to bring their boards to the front. Discuss the different ways of working out the answer. Get some learners to invent another rectangle problem for the class to try. Involving the class and finding out who understands is crucial.

	4	5
2	8	10
3	12	15

Area 45 cm²

Possible answers on boards:

Area = 8 + 10 + 12 + 15 = 45 cm² or

Area = 2 × 4 + 2 × 5 + 3 × 4 + 3 × 5 = 45 cm²

Area = 5 × 9 = 45 cm²

Area = (2 + 3)(4 + 5) = 5 × 9 = 45 cm²

Now the learners need to be brave to try to write this area involving x in two ways.

Answers: Area = $x^2 + 3x + 2x + 6$ or Area = $(x + 2)(x + 3)$

Give diagrams for $6(x + 2)$, etc. Answers on showboards.

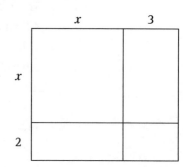

Activity 2: Multiplying out brackets – using grids

- Showboards if possible

Pairs and whole class   *50 minutes*

What the teacher is doing

1. Fill in this multiplication table.

×	4	3
2	8	
3		

Add the four numbers in the table.

Now **show me** your answer.

2. Draw a multiplication grid. Choose any numbers you like for the top and side of your grid and work out the total.

3. Can anyone find another grid where the total has a factor of 5?

When you have lots of grids where the total has a factor of 5 on the board ask what the learners notice about the starting numbers and the totals.

4. At the start of the next lesson the teacher can challenge the learners to fill in a grid with x.

×	x	2
x	x^2	
3		

And record the total.

What the learners are doing

1.

×	4	3
2	8	6
3	12	9

Total = 8 + 6 + 12 + 9 = 35

2. Learners choose any starting numbers

×	2	6
3	6	18
7	14	42

×	3	4
2	6	8
4	12	16

Total: 80   Total: 42

3. Trying grids. Any learner who finds another grid with a factor of 5 puts in on the class board.

Possible explanations:

You always have 2 and 3 in the top or the side.

No you can have 1 and 4 as well.

When you add the side numbers it goes into the total.

4.

×	x	2
x	x^2	2x
3	3x	6

$(x + 3)(x + 2) = x^2 + 2x + 3x + 6$
$= x^2 + 5x + 6$

Teaching ideas

- You want to get as many learners involved as possible. If a learner who usually struggles finds a total with a factor of 5 be sure to ask them to write it on the board. Having lots of grids on the board makes it easier to see the patterns.
- It can be hard to put the patterns into words. Try asking a learner to the board so they can point at the numbers. Let many learners speak until the explanations become clearer.

  Extend to grids with negative numbers. Will the total of these grids have a factor of 5?

×	6	−1
2		
4		

×	7	−4
8		
−3		

- Everyone can join in to search for grids with a factor of 5. The learners see that adding the side numbers gives a factor of the total. This helps them to understand how the grid can be used for the abstract idea of $(x + 3)(x + 2) = x^2 + 5x + 6$

Changes in my classroom practice

Implementing the teaching strategies

Discussion	*see page 8*

Getting the learners involved

Algebraic manipulation can seem abstract and pointless. To avoid this you need to get the whole class involved and active. Drawing the area diagrams with numbers and the grids with numbers is accessible to everyone in the class, which is why it is a good place to start. You want to build the confidence of your learners before moving to algebra. The purpose of the activities is that learners understand not just *how* to multiply out brackets as a technique to be remembered but understand *why* the method works and *why* you always get four terms.

Getting feedback

How do you know if you have been successful in getting all the learners to understand? The individual showboards are very useful for getting responses from all the learners in the class. They can transform your teaching and are arguably essential when teaching large classes.

Which of these choices are possible for you?

- *Getting the school to buy commercially produced plastic showboards with erasable whiteboard marker pens.*
  You can store these in plastic bags with a pen and a scrap of material or piece of sponge as a wiper. The learners **must** get in the habit of replacing the pen top after use.

- *Making your own showboards.*
  Photocopy the sheet of squared paper on page **100**. Photocopy on one side only so your showboard has one plain and one squared side. Laminate the paper. You will need to make a class set and store in plastic bags with pens as above.

- *Using a large pile of A4 paper that has been used only on one side.*
  Learners can fold paper into 8 and use to answer 8 questions. This works best with marker pens because it is easier for teacher to read.

If you don't have showboards there are many things you can do. You can bring learners to the board. You can circulate the classroom checking what a sample of learners have written – though this gets harder for large classes. You can ask yes/no questions, e.g. look at this statement:

$$(-2) \times (-x) = -2x$$

Put up your **left** hand if you think that the statement is **False**, put up your **right** hand up if you think it is **True**.

Key questions to develop understanding

When the learners are using rectangles and grids to expand brackets:

- What numbers did you multiply to get this answer?
- What is the same about these two grids? What is different?
- Explain to me how you worked it out with just numbers not letters.

Follow up activity

Difference of squares

When you are planning to teach a topic you can look for a variety of approaches:

- visual images
- practical approaches
- presentation and discussion

Draw a square 10 cm by 10 cm. Cut out a square 4 cm × 4 cm from a corner.

So you are left with an L-shape of area $10^2 - 4^2$. This is a picture of the difference of two squares.

Cut the L-shape into two trapeziums.

Can you fit the two trapeziums together to make a rectangle?

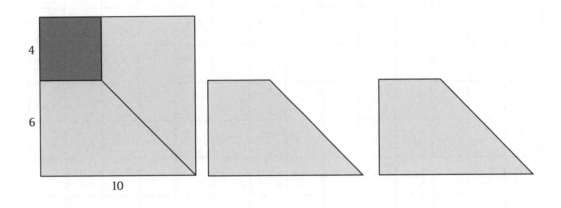

Label the sides of the rectangle you have made with the lengths.

What is the area of the rectangle? $6 \times (10 + 4) = 6 \times 14$

The L-shape and the rectangle have the same area. $10^2 - 4^2 = 6 \times 14$

Try this for a square $a \times a$ with a $b \times b$ square cut out and you will see how this links with the algebraic formula for the difference of squares.

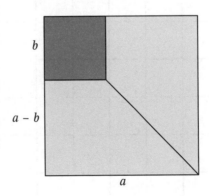

Worksheet

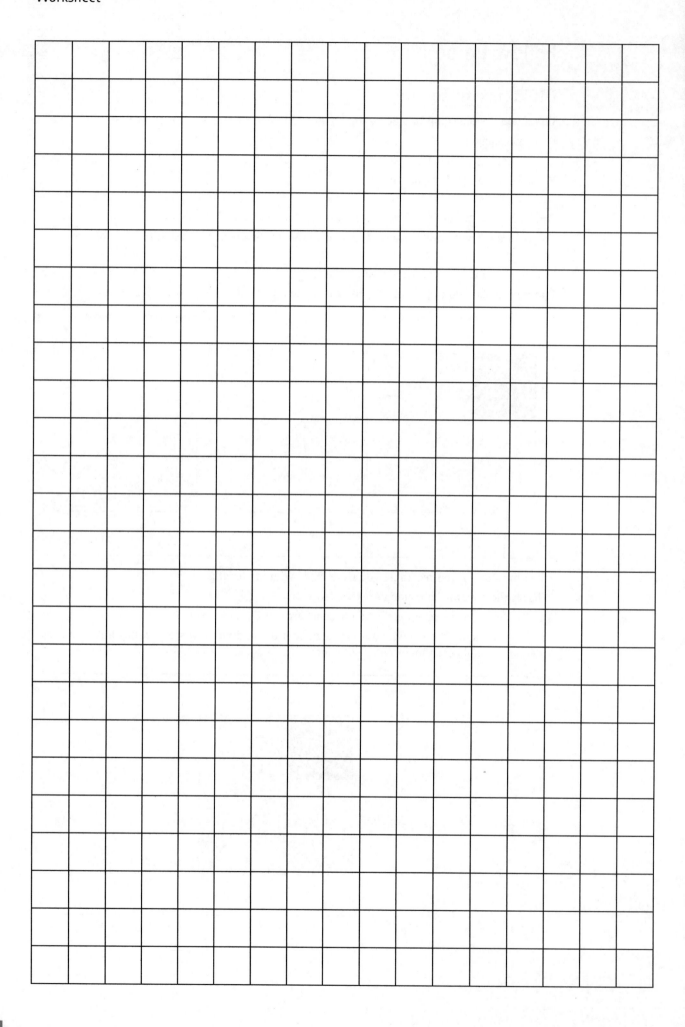

Chapter 12

Introducing angles

Teaching strategy: Visual and People Maths

Curriculum content

Angle as rotation. Angles on parallel lines, in triangles and polygons

Prior knowledge needed

Familiarity with shapes; can be used to introduce or to review knowledge of angles.

Intended Learning Outcomes

At the end of this activity teachers and learners will:

- Know properties of angles on parallel lines, triangles and polygons
- Understand angle is an amount of turn
- Be able to estimate the size of angles and use angle properties to find unknown angles
- Appreciate how geometrical facts can be derived from simpler geometrical facts
- Have experienced turning though angles and interpreting diagrams involving angles

Fact box

One whole turn is 360°.

Angles on a straight line add up to 180°.

Angles on parallel lines

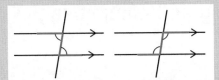

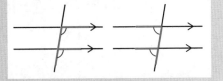

Alternate angles are equal.

Corresponding angles are equal.

Angles in a triangle add up to 180°.

Exterior angles of any polygon add up to 360°.

For a regular polygon all the sides and all the angles are the same.

Exterior angles of a regular polygon with n sides are $\frac{360}{n}$ degrees.

Interior angles of a regular polygon with n sides are $\frac{180 - 360}{n}$ degrees.

Resources for this workshop

Straws; A4 paper; pencils; compasses or circular object; protractors; two large sheets of paper for triangles; sticky tape; scissors.

Workshop Activities for Teachers

Activity 1: Estimating angles

> • Straws; A4 paper; pencils; compasses or circular object
> *Pairs, whole group*   *30 minutes*

Making resources

Follow instructions on pages **107** & **108** to make angle estimators from straws and from paper. Decide which are most convenient for you to use to demonstrate to the whole class and for learners to use. Share ideas on storing practical resources.

Planning

Read through Classroom Activity 1 and discuss how you can emphasise angle as an amount of turn and explain to learners why it was decided to describe one whole turn as 360°.

Teaching

Take it in turns to be the teacher and direct the group in Classroom Activity 1. Who was most skilful in getting you to estimate and to remember vocabulary?

> **Notes**
> • There can be quite long gaps between lessons on geometry so learners are particularly likely to forget vocabulary. These simple activities will remind learners of previous work on angles.
> • 360 seems a strange number. Historians think that the early use of angles was linked to astronomy. An estimate of how long it took the earth to turn around the sun was 360 days so it was decided to divide a whole turn into 360 degrees.

Activity 2: Identifying and naming angles on parallel lines

> • Two sticks or pencils
> *Individual, whole group*   *30 minutes*

Everyone should draw a grid with two sets of parallel lines.

Choose any angle and mark it in red.

Now mark all the angles which LOOK the same as your chosen angle.

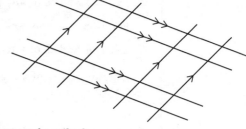

Choose another colour and repeat until all the angles are marked.

Discuss whether it is possible to guess which angles are described as opposite angles.

Demonstrate with two sticks that **opposite** angles are the same

Hold the sticks in the middle and open them out to an X shape.

How do you help learners remember which angles are alternate and which corresponding?

> **Notes**
> **Seeing** the angles and **naming** the angles.
>
> It is surprising how many angles are the same. Only two colours are needed. Although learners often find it hard to remember the names opposite, alternating and corresponding, all learners seem to be able to **see** the angles which are the same. Thinking of the letter Z for alternating angles and F for corresponding angles can be helpful. Though the learners have to look for back-to-front Fs and back-to-front Zs as well. **Look** before starting work.

Activity 3: Angles in a triangle

* Paper for triangles; sticky tape; scissors

Individual, whole group   *30 minutes*

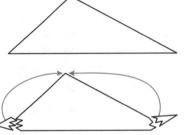

Choose one person to be the teacher. They need to put two sheets of paper together and cut out two **scalene** triangles the same size – large enough to be seen from the back of the class.

Stick one of the triangles to the board with sticky tape.

Show that your second triangle is exactly the same size.

Cut off angles A and C with a zig-zag cut. (The zig-zag makes clear which is the angle and which is the cut.)

Fix the three parts of the triangle to the board as in the diagram.

Now we want to fit all three angles together at the top of the triangle.

Turn the pieces and fit them together.

Show with a ruler that the three pieces fit to make a straight line.

Everyone in the group can now try this for themselves. However simple a process seems it is always helpful to actually try it yourself before going into class to see if there are any pitfalls. (When I tried it without zigzags the learners made straight cuts and couldn't remember which was the angle and which was the cut!)

This is a vivid demonstration that the angles of a triangle add up to 180°.

It is **not** a proof because we can't be certain that the line is exactly straight.

Use this now to try to work out a formal proof instead of cutting the paper.

> **Notes**
> Start with the triangle. Label the vertices.
>
> Draw a line parallel to the base through the top vertex.
>
> Now look for an angle the same as angle B... and an angle the same as angle C.

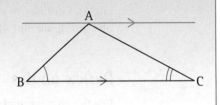

Classroom Activities for Learners

Activity 1: Angle as an amount of turn

- Large angle estimator and smaller estimators for each learner (see page **107**)
- Protractors

Whole class, pairs   *50 minutes*

Estimating angles

Ask learners to stand and face the right-hand side of the classroom holding their right hand straight out in front of them. Give a series of instructions for turning anticlockwise:

- Quarter turn left, another quarter turn left, half-turn left.
- A third of a turn left, another third of a turn, etc.

Ask learners to sit down and discuss how angles are measured and that a whole turn is taken as 360°. Now ask the learners to stand again and give instructions for turning anticlockwise in degrees:

- Turn 90° anticlockwise, 180° another 90°. Learners should be back where they started.
- Turn 60° another 30°, 90°, 180°
- Turn 120°, 60° , 60°, 120°

Using straw angle estimators to show angles that make up 180° (supplementary angles)

Hold up your large angle estimator (made from sticks or two rulers). Choose an angle, e.g. 120°. Hold the two arms together. Slowly open the arms. The class must softly call STOP when you get to 120°. Repeat with different angles until learners are confident with estimating angles.

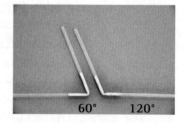

In pairs. First learner writes down an obtuse angle and sets angle estimators to show the obtuse angle. Second learner must write down the angle needed to make 180° and set the estimators to that angle.

Measuring with a protractor

Use a large board protractor (if available) to introduce or remind learners about measuring angles. Continue to use the angle estimator on top of the protractor to emphasise that you are measuring amount of turn.

Reflex angles

Use the circular angle indicators to demonstrate reflex angles. In pairs ask the learners to use two circular indicators to show angles that add to 360°.

Activity 2: Angles on parallel lines and in a triangle

- Two large triangles for teacher; paper and scissors for each pair

Whole class, pairs   *50 minutes*

Use the activities described in the teacher workshops to introduce angles on parallel lines and angles in a triangle.

Activity 3: Angles in polygons using People Maths

- Open space indoors or out
- Showboards; long string or rope (5 or 6 metres)

Individual, whole class   *50 minutes*

Ask 5 learners to stand inside the rope holding it with their fingers to make a 5-sided polygon Now ask a learner to stand in the middle of a side with their right-hand straight out in front of them. They now walk around the rope, turning at each corner to face the person at the next corner. Repeat this, noting the direction in which the walker was facing at first and then how far round they have turned by the time they get back to the starting position.

The walker should have completed **one whole turn.** We chose an irregular 5-sided polygon. Would making it a regular polygon (all the sides the same length) change anything? Would having more or fewer sides make a difference?

If there are some doubts here, repeat the activity with another polygon. This activity shows that the **sum of the exterior angles of any polygon is 360°**. It also gives us a method of finding the exterior angle of any regular polygon; divide 360° by the number of sides.

How can we find the interior angle? (You know that a half turn is 180°.)

Copy and complete a table showing the interior and exterior angle of the following regular polygons:

Calculating interior and exterior angles of regular polygons

	Number of sides	Exterior angle	Interior angle
Equilateral triangle	3	120°	60°
Square	4	90°	90°
Regular pentagon	5		
Regular hexagon			
Regular octagon			
Regular nonagon			
Regular decagon			

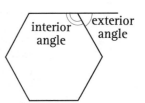

interior angle   exterior angle

Changes in my classroom practice

Implementing the teaching strategy

Visual learning styles   *see page 4*
People maths   *see page 5*

Visualisation

Geometry is a very visual topic and the activities in this chapter encourage learners to stop and look. Discuss the many small ways in which teachers can encourage learners to notice the important features of a diagram, e.g. use of colour.

Kinaesthetic learning

In kinaesthetic learning the learners carry out physical activities. Learning to ride a bike is kinaesthetic learning. In these activities the learners actually turn through angles to give them a vivid sense of the size of the angle. It only takes a few minutes but it is memorable. Can you think of a way of including kinaesthetic activities in the topics you will be teaching in the next few weeks? Count it as a success whenever you get the learners up out of their seats and involved in the maths!

Reasoning

Reasoning is at the heart of mathematics and in geometry learners start with some basic knowledge of shapes and angles and derive more and more facts by reasoning. Look at this proof that the angles in a triangle add up to 180° and see how knowledge of angles on parallel lines and straight lines is used to build knowledge of the angle sum of a triangle. As your learners continue to study mathematics they will come to understand formal proofs with a **reason** for each **statement**.

STATEMENT	REASON
$< B_1 = < A_1$	Alternate angles XY parallel to BC
$< C_1 = < A_3$	Alternate angles XY parallel to BC
$< A_1 + < A_2 + < A_3 = 180°$	Angles on a straight line

So $< B_1 + < A_2 + < C_1 = 180°$

The angles of a triangle add up to 180°!!!

You can help your learners get started on the idea of proof by always asking **Why?**

Make sure you are always asking for a **reason**.

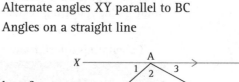

Estimating

Estimating is making a sensible guess. We do it all the time in deciding how much food we should buy or how long it will take us to get into town. In mathematics lessons learners can be reluctant to guess as they see mathematics as something which is either right or wrong. Estimating is particularly useful before measuring angles as if we estimate 120° and then read 58° from our protractor we will sense that something is wrong. It is that ability to correct themselves that you are trying to develop in your learners. Encourage your learners to think that being a good guesser is a useful skill! Try this activity.

In pairs one learner draws an angle and writes beside it their estimate. The other learner measures the angle. The first learner is successful if their estimate is within 10° initially. Later the estimates must be within 5°.

Estimate	150°	
Measurement	158°	Success!

Key questions to develop understanding

- Can you see another angle that **looks** the same?
- Is there a **reason** those angles are the same?
- Can you estimate the size of the angle?

Errors and misconceptions

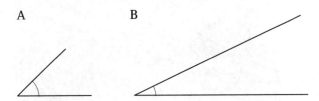

Is angle A or B larger? In a research study a surprising number of children replied B. It was thought that the longer lines and larger amount of space between the lines influenced the response. Since this research the curriculum and most textbooks emphasise that angle is an amount of turn and not a diagram on a page. The activities in this chapter show many ways to demonstrate in the classroom that angle is an amount of turn.

Helping learners remember

1. Give groups of 4 learners a sheet of A4 paper. Ask them to think of all the geometrical facts they have just learnt. Write the facts on the board. Ask the learners to choose one piece of information and construct a clear, colourful diagram to communicate the information.

2. Work with the learners to list the names of polygons and ideas for remembering the number of sides.

Quadrilateral	4 sides	Quads means 4 children
Pentagon	5 sides	An aerial picture of the Pentagon in the USA?
Hexagon	6 sides	
Septagon or Heptagon	7 sides	
Octagon	8 sides	An octopus has 8 legs
Nonagon	9 sides	
Decagon	10 sides	A decade is 10 years

Historical note: September, October, November, December used to be the 7th, 8th, 9th and 10th months of the year. Then Julius Caesar, the Roman Emperor changed the calendar by adding two months July (for Julius) and August (for Augustus). So now December which sounds like the 10th month is the 12th month.

Making resources

Different ways to make angle estimators

1. From drinking straws

   You need: drinking straws and some paper.

   Take two drinking straws. Scrunch up a piece of paper and push it into the end of both straws to fix them together at one end. The learners can use this to estimate angles and hold up to show the teacher.

   If you can't find straws you can use two pencils or two rulers to demonstrate turning through an angle.

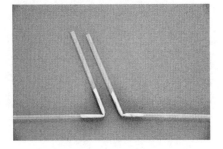

2. Circular angle indicators from paper

You need: white paper and coloured paper. Magazine paper will do or white paper coloured in.

Draw circles either with compasses or by drawing around a circular object. Cut out two circles one from white paper and one from coloured paper. Mark the centre of each circle draw a radius and **cut** along the radius.

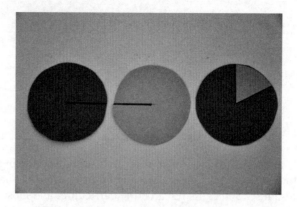

Slot the two circles together along the cuts you have just made. Turn the circles to show the white angle of the bottom circle. Now give instructions, e.g. show me 90°, show me 120°. These indicators are particularly useful for **reflex** angles.

The important thing is that everyone in the class estimates and demonstrates the angles. Keep the measures to use during mental maths sessions and regularly get the learners to estimate angles until they become skilled.

2D shapes

Teaching strategy: Questioning and discussion in pairs

Curriculum content

Identify a range of 2-dimensional shapes and begin to understand their properties

Prior knowledge needed

Some experience with basic shapes, angles and parallel lines

Intended Learning Outcomes

At the end of this activity teachers and learners will:

- Know a range of mathematics vocabulary relating to 2-dimensional shapes
- Understand that it is important to be able to *analyse* and *explain* in mathematics
- Be able to describe and put into categories a range of 2-dimensional shapes
- Appreciate the importance of precise definitions and descriptions
- Have experience of describing 2D shapes precisely

Fact box

Polygons are 2-dimensional closed shapes with straight sides:

- Triangles have 3 sides
- Quadrilaterals have 4 sides
- Pentagons have 5 sides
- Hexagons have 6 sides
- Octagons have 8 sides

Polygons are regular if all their sides and all their angles are equal.

Some special triangles are **equilateral, isosceles, right-angled and obtuse-angled triangles.**

A triangle with no equal sides is called a scalene triangle.

Some special quadrilaterals are **squares, rectangles, rhombuses, trapeziums, parallelograms.**

Circles have a fixed radius (distance from the centre to the circumference); the diameter goes through the centre and is twice the length of the radius.

A semi-circle is exactly half a circle.

Resources for this workshop

Photocopy of grid on page 116 for each pair; scissors; showboards; a mathematical dictionary would be useful. You can find one online at http://www.lancsngfl.ac.uk/secondary/math/download/file/PDF/Maths%20Glossary.pdf

Workshop Activities for Teachers

Activity 1: Matching shapes to their properties

> • Photocopy of grid on page **116** for each pair
> • Scissors
>
> *Pairs or groups of 3*   *30 minutes*

In groups of 2 or 3, make a list of the mathematical words your learners need to know to describe 2D shapes. Now choose between 12 and 20 words that you think will be most useful for them to focus on and make a list to display on the wall.

Photocopy the grid on page **116** or fold two sheets of A4 paper into 8. Draw a picture of a shape in one box and write one or two properties of this shape in the other box using some words from your list. (Sometimes the property you write may be matched to more than one shape.) For example, you could draw a picture of an isosceles triangle marked:

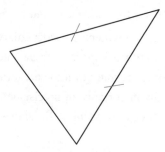

and in the other box you could say 'a triangle with 2 equal sides'.

Cut your cards up, muddle them up. Swap with another group of teachers and see if you can match up their cards.

Think: how you might improve your set of cards, given your experience. If you have time, make a better, or harder, or easier set.

> **Notes**
> • Choose vocabulary that builds on what your learners know and what they need to know. See also a list of ideas on page **114**.
>
> • Why is it helpful to sometimes draw pictures in unusual ways, e.g. a square
>
>   as ?
>
> • To know you have a regular polygon, do you need to know all the angles *and* all the sides are equal, or will just one of those do? Why (not)?
>
> • In a class, you might suggest that each set made by a group is marked in some way (with a picture or colour or initials), so a set can be kept together and perhaps used at the beginning of the next lesson.
>
> • Notice how making your own cards, rather than just using ones that someone else has made, makes you think hard about what the words mean.

Activity 2: Photograph my picture

> • Pens and paper
>
> *Pairs or groups of 3*   *30 minutes*

Work in a group of 2 (or 3, if you would like more practice): try different groupings from Activity 1.

Divide a sheet of paper into 2 parts. In one part you are going to draw a picture which you partner(s) will have to draw from your description, without seeing it.

Think of a picture which uses basic mathematical shapes, and which you could describe using mathematical vocabulary of shape, size and position. Try to make it challenging but not too complicated, for example, you might draw.

 (Other suggestions are given in the lesson activities that follow these pages). One teacher now describes the picture to the other(s), without them being able to see the picture. How similar can they make it? The teacher giving instructions should not be able to see what is being drawn.

 Now swop so the other teacher gives instructions.

 Who do you think has to work harder in this activity, the teacher doing the describing or the teacher doing the drawing? How could you make the activity harder (or easier)? What sorts of mathematical thinking do you use? *Talk about* which shapes are good ones to use.

> **Notes**
> This is hard, and gets harder still if no questions are allowed: it might be an idea to try it the first time with questions allowed, and then for the second teacher's drawing do not allow any questions. *Challenge* each other so there's a real sense of achievement!

Activity 3: Alternative introduction

> *Pairs and whole group*   *30 minutes*

 Read through and discuss Activity 2 in the classroom activities. Take it in turns to act as teacher and introduce the activities. If you have time, work together through the discussion on page **115** about whether a square is a rectangle. This question often comes up in a lesson on 2D shapes and it is good to prepare yourself by discussing with colleagues – it usually generates some good mathematical argument!

Classroom Activities for Learners

Activity 1: Introduction and Shape Pairs

> • Scissors; showboards; scrap card or paper
>
> *Pairs or groups of 3*   *15 + 30 minutes*

Introduction

- Ask the learners to give some names of 2-dimensional shapes. Write each word on the board. For each, ask the learners to draw it on a showboard, then ask one learner to describe what makes that shape special (*or* ask a learner to come to main board and draw the shape).
- Make a list of what makes the shape special on the board. Ask the rest of the class if they agree. Encourage them to discuss, to change, to add ideas and to make links to other shapes.

This discussion is *formative assessment* of what learners already understand, and also reminds them what they know.

Main Activity

- This is the same as Teacher Workshop Activity 1: use list of words on the board, or ask learners to choose their own, remembering they want to challenge their friends!
- In 2s or 3s, ask learners to make a set of pairs of cards; then swop with another group to match up.
- Ask learners to decide if there's anything they want to change on the cards they made, to make them better.
- Ask learners what they now know better.

Activity 2: Alternative introduction to Activity 1

> • Showboards

Alternative introduction

- Ask the learners to think of a 2D shape (not telling anyone their idea).
- Choose learners to ask questions about the property of a shape, for example, learner 1 can ask the class "Does your shape have parallel sides?" Learner 2 could ask "Does your shape have a right angle?"
- Ask all learners to write the answers for their shape on their showboards, e.g. My secret shape has: Parallel sides, No right angles.
- After 3 or 4 questions, choose a learner to stand at the front holding up their showboard. Ask the class to guess their shape from the properties. Other learners with the same shape put up their hands.
- After a time any learner whose shape has not been identified gives clues (properties) until the class guess the shape.

> **Teaching ideas**
>
> Activity 2 helps learners think about what sorts of properties they need to use. They may not find this easy the first time they play but it will get more familiar if repeated.

Activity 3: Made Up 'Photographs' of Shapes

- A simple picture prepared on sheet of paper for you to describe to the class
- Showboards or paper

Whole class and pairs   *30 minutes*

Teacher gives instructions

Draw a simple picture on a sheet of paper but **don't let the class see**. Tell the class that you are going to describe the picture and they must try to draw exactly what you say so that they will have a photograph of your picture. Give instructions slowly and allow learners to ask questions if they are not sure.

Ask everyone to hold up their picture and then show the picture you were describing. Discuss what was difficult and what helps to make instructions clear.

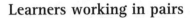

Learners working in pairs

Ask one person in each pair to draw a very simple picture including at least two mathematical shapes. Tell them to keep it hidden. Now describe the shape to your partner. Try to give very clear instructions. Partner draws the shape.

Now the partner must draw a hidden picture and describe it. When the learners are drawing very good 'photographs' suggest that no questions are allowed. This makes drawing much harder.

Changes in my classroom practice

Implementing the teaching strategy

| Questioning | see page 7 |
| Discussion | see page 8 |

- It is not very interesting to just have a list of definitions to learn, so *talking* about shapes, and using pictures can help.
- These activities make learners take part in an active way that sounds easy, but teachers should try themselves because both activities are harder than they look.
- Thinking rigorously is challenging for young people (and adults!), but *talking* as they do so (with a range of other learners over time) helps them realise what is needed.
- The list of words used on the cards depends on the background knowledge and the curriculum: learners will learn most if there are some cards they can match quite easily, but others that are new to them or hard to do.

Helping learners remember

Words for describing 2D shapes are often hard to remember and even harder to spell. Understanding what is meant by words, such as parallel, can take time and explaining words for themselves will take longer. Learners can make a dictionary to hang on the wall and share. It can be used to check the spelling of difficult words, for example, parallel, rhombus or isosceles.

Illustrations can be included in the dictionary and new words can be added when the learners meet them.

Learners love to see their own creations so a poster for the wall or a book made up from the different 'photographs' will keep them talking for several days. Get them to label parts of the photographs to reinforce the words they need to remember.

Words for learners to include in their dictionary:

- side, line, angle, vertex, vertices, corner, straight, curved, circular, horizontal, parallel, perpendicular, vertical, diagonal, intersecting
- acute angle, right angle, obtuse angle, reflex angle
- bigger, longer, taller, shorter, narrow, wide
- symmetrical, line symmetry, rotational symmetry, mirror line, axis of symmetry, center of rotation
- circle, diameter, circumference, radius, semi-circle, arc
- regular, irregular.

Follow up activities

Find the wrong answers

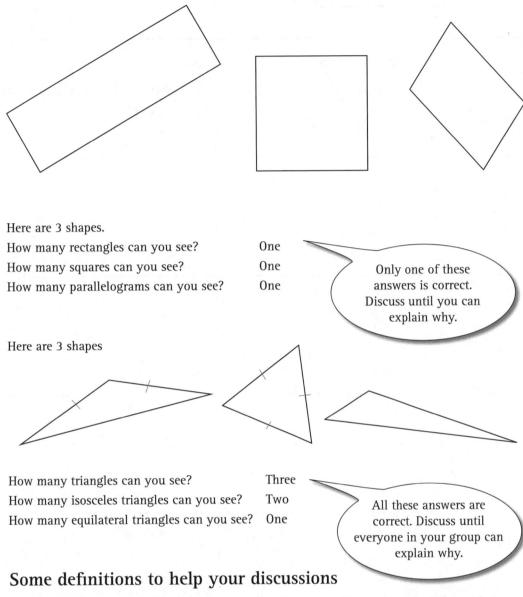

Here are 3 shapes.

How many rectangles can you see?   One

How many squares can you see?   One

How many parallelograms can you see?   One

> Only one of these answers is correct. Discuss until you can explain why.

Here are 3 shapes

How many triangles can you see?   Three

How many isosceles triangles can you see?   Two

How many equilateral triangles can you see?   One

> All these answers are correct. Discuss until everyone in your group can explain why.

Some definitions to help your discussions

- A rectangle is a quadrilateral with two pairs of opposite sides equal and all the angles are right angles.
- A square is a quadrilateral with all the sides the same length and all the angles are right-angles. (Can you see that a square fits the definition for a rectangle because it has two pairs of opposite sides equal? So although it may sound strange a square is a rectangle!)
- An isosceles triangle is a triangle with two sides equal.
- An equilateral triangle is a triangle with three sides equal.

So why is an equilateral triangle also isosceles?

A triangle is isosceles if you can find two equal sides. It doesn't matter if the other side is equal as well! It makes sense to mathematicians to include as many shapes as possible in a definition so if you prove a fact for all isosceles triangles you don't have to prove it all over again for equilateral triangles. The equilateral triangles are included in your proof. If you meet one person from South Africa and one from the Eastern Cape you meet two South Africans.

	A shape with 2 pairs of equal angles
	A 3 sided shape with 2 equal angles (or more!)

Transformations and tessellations

Teaching strategy: Visual and practical, People maths

Curriculum content

Recognise, describe and perform translations, reflections and rotations on geometric figures and shapes

Prior knowledge needed

There are 360° in a whole turn and 90° in a quarter-turn (a right angle). Vocabulary: perpendicular, quadrilateral, parallelogram.

Intended Learning Outcomes

At the end of this activity teachers and learners will:

- Know what is meant by a translation, a rotation and a reflection
- Understand that after a reflection, an object and its image are equal distances from the mirror line
- Be able to justify why quadrilaterals and triangles will tessellate
- Appreciate that combining quadrilaterals and triangles in a tessellation can lead to discovering angle facts about them
- Have experienced some aesthetic patterning possibilities of mathematics through tessellation

Fact box

A transformation is a movement of a shape in the plane that transforms the shape into its image.

A translation moves the object along a straight path without turning it.

A reflection in a mirror line flips the shape over so that the image is an equal distance from the mirror line. Each point of the object gives an image point the same distance from the mirror line. The line from the image point to the object point is perpendicular to the mirror.

A rotation about a point turns the object keeping it an equal distance from this point (the center of rotation).

The centre of rotation may be within the shape, on the edge of the shape or outside the shape.

Congruent shapes are the same shape and the same size.

Corresponding points on two congruent shapes will lie exactly on top of each other when one shape covers the other.

A shape is said to tessellate the plane if congruent copies of the one shape fit together without any spaces between them in a pattern that can be extended to infinity in all directions.

The sum of adjacent angles on a straight line add up to 180°.

The sum of the angles in a quadrilateral add up to 360°.

Resources for this workshop

Scissors; scrap card; squared paper; mirrors (home made from foil and card); sticks; string; ruler; a photocopy of page 124 for each pair; tracing paper.

Workshop Activities for Teachers

Activity 1: Translations and rotations

- Scissors; scrap card; squared paper; tracing paper
- Photocopy of page 124

Pairs, whole group   *30 minutes*

Translation

Working in pairs cut out a cardboard quadrilateral making sure the edges are straight. Mark the corners A, B, C and D. On squared paper draw around the quadrilateral and mark the drawing 'object'.

Now **translate** the quadrilateral along 7 squares horizontally and up 4 squares **without turning it**. Draw around the quadrilateral and mark the drawing 'image 1'. This translation can be described as $(x, y) \rightarrow (x + 7, y + 4)$ as for each point on the object the x-coordinate is increased by 7 and the y-coordinate is increased by 4.

Rotation

Starting again with the quadrilateral in the 'object' position, **rotate** the quadrilateral a quarter turn anti-clockwise and place it down somewhere on the squared paper. Draw around it and mark this drawing as 'image 2'. (See photocopy of page 124).

Take tracing paper and trace the 'object'. Now put the point of a pencil or a drawing pin where you think the centre of rotation might be. When you rotate about this point does the 'object' rotate onto the 'image 2'. If not try rotating about a different point until you are successful. A rotation can be described by giving the centre of rotation and the angle turned.

Activity 2: Tessellations of a quadrilateral

- Scissors; scrap card

Pairs, whole group   *30 minutes*

Use a cardboard quadrilateral as a template and draw around it in the centre of a blank sheet of paper. (Don't make the quadrilateral too small or it will take too long to fill the paper.) Now using only translations and rotations (i.e. do not flip the shape over) try to cover the whole sheet without leaving any gaps and without any overlaps. It should be possible to continue the pattern in every direction even beyond the edges of the paper. This will be a **tessellation** of the quadrilateral.

What can you say about the angles of the quadrilateral?

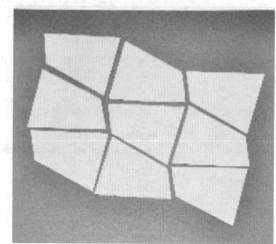

There are different ways to get from one position of the quadrilateral to another. Investigate the effect of a half-turn followed by another half turn.

Activity 3: Reflections

- Mirrors (home made from foil and card)
- Sticks; string; ruler; scissors; scrap card

3s, whole group   *30 minutes*

Reflections with people

 Place a stick on the floor to represent
the mirror line. With a partner on either side of the mirror line, one person is the **object** the
other is the *image* and must mirror the object. Now the object raises a hand and the image
must mirror the action.

 Hold a **piece of string** tightly between each pair of teachers (one holding with the left hand
and the other with the right hand). Notice that the string is at right-angles to the mirror. The
object can move their hand around. The *image* mirrors the movement. Notice that the string is
always **perpendicular** to the mirror. The distance from each hand to the mirror is the same.

Reflections in a mirror

Cut out a cardboard scalene triangle. Make sure the edges are straight and the triangle *is not*
right angled or isosceles or equilateral. Label the vertices A, B and C.

Draw a diagonal mirror line on the paper and place the
cardboard triangle on one side of the mirror line. Draw around
the triangle. Now flip the triangle over (the labels will now
be on the under-side). Try to place the flipped triangle so that
it shows the reflection of the triangle you have drawn on the
paper. Use the mirror to help by placing it on the mirror line
and moving it until the *image* you see of the original triangle
lies on the flipped triangle.

Measure the distance from the mirror line to a point on the
'object'.

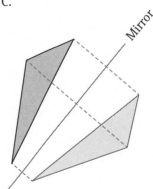

 Measure the distance from the mirror line to a corresponding
point on the 'image' to show that the distances are the same.

Using transformations to tessellate a triangle

Now use your triangle to make a tessellation covering a whole blank sheet of paper. See
what happens when you use reflections. What happens when you use only rotations and
translations?

Classroom Activities for Learners

Activity 1: Translations and rotations

> • Chalk; scissors; scrap card; string; rulers
>
> *Pairs, whole group* *60 minutes*

Try to find a space with a tiled floor or square paving stones. Mark the direction of the x- and y-axes. The learner holds a large cardboard quadrilateral horizontally and moves keeping the quadrilateral quite straight.

Translations

Have one learner stand and mark his/her position on the floor with a letter A. Ask this learner to take 2 steps in the direction of the x-axis. (Don't turn the quadrilateral!) Mark the new position B. Explain the vocabulary that this is a translation $x \to x + 2$ from position A to position B.

Now ask the learner to move 4 steps from position B in the y-direction. That is $y \to y + 4$. Mark the new position C. Ask other learners to give directions using the formal language, e.g. please do the translation $y \to y - 3$. (The symbol $\to$ is read as 'goes to'.)

Rotations

One learner holds one end of a length of string. Tie the other end (to a door knob or table leg). Now the learner moves so that the string remains taut. The fixed end is the **centre of rotation** and the learner is rotating about this centre. Ask the other learners what angle the learner has moved through.

Starting back in the first position, keeping the centre of rotation fixed and the string taut, get the learner to do three 60 turns. With 5 learners and 5 pieces of string fixed at the centre of rotation ask the learners to position themselves equally spaced around in a circle and talk about the angle of rotation needed to get from each position to the next. What would the angle of rotation be if there were 8 or 9 learners?

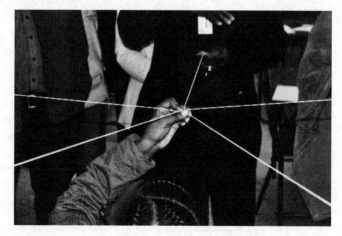

In the classroom

Using rulers, pairs of learners first cut cardboard **quadrilaterals** (which are not squares or rectangles) making sure the edges are straight. On a blank piece of paper draw around the shape. Mark the middle of one edge and rotate the shape around this point giving it a half-turn. Draw around the new position. Now using only half-turns about different edges make a **tessellation** leaving no gaps and no overlaps.

Teaching ideas

- Learners may have difficulty doing half-turns about the middle of one edge (without flipping it over). They are correct if the edges fit together exactly with the middles matching.
- If the learners colour or shade one side of their quadrilateral it will be clearer when it has been reflected (flipped over).
- Each different angle of the quadrilateral can be marked with a different symbol or with a letter. When the learners have completed a few images point out that any point where 4 quadrilaterals meet has the 4 different angles. This shows that the angles of a quadrilateral (any quadrilateral) add up to 360°.

Activity 2: Reflections

- Scissors; scrap card

Pairs, whole group   *20 minutes*

Ask a pair of learners to stand facing each other about a metre apart. Ask the first learner to raise their left arm. The second learner will act as if they are in a mirror and raise the hand that looks like the reflection. Discuss the fact that the reflected arm is the opposite (right) arm.

Mark with chalk or with a stick where the mirror would be. Now ask the first learner to take one step back – away from the mirror. How will the second learner move to keep the reflection correct?

Ask one of these learners to move one leg away from the mirror line. Ask the class what must the other learner do to keep the image correct?

Now sitting down, get the learners to cut out a cardboard triangle and mark the vertices A, B and C. On squared paper draw around the triangle labelling the vertices A, B and C the same as the cardboard triangle. Mark on the paper a mirror line and flip the cardboard shape over and position it as the image. Emphasise that all corresponding parts of the image must be an equal distance from the mirror.

Investigate different mirror lines: horizontal, vertical and diagonal.

What happens when the mirror line lies along one of the edges of the triangle?

What happens when the mirror line cuts across the triangle (this is possible on paper).

On a blank sheet of paper make a tessellation of the triangle discussing the moves from one position to the next. Identify translations, rotations and reflections identifying the centres and angles of rotation and the mirror lines for reflections.

Use colours to make a wall display of the different patterns that can be made.

Teaching ideas

- Selecting learners who 'match' in shape and size will emphasise the idea of a reflection.
- Using one edge of the triangle as the mirror line and reflecting (flipping the triangle keeping this edge fixed) makes a quadrilateral. Some learners may tessellate this quadrilateral.
- Giving the triangle a half-turn about the centre of one edge will result in a parallelogram. Tessellating this parallelogram will give a different pattern.

Changes in my classroom practice

Implementing the teaching strategies

Visual and practical learning styles	*see page 4*
People maths	*see page 5*

People maths

You need to identify a place in or near your school that is good for People Math activities. You may be able to

- Move desks in your classroom to clear a space
- Move with the learners to a corridor or hall
- Find an outside space.

It is sometimes useful to be able to make temporary marks on the floor either with chalk, or by taping paper to the floor. A trail of sand works well for marking a grass area.

Developing the language

'Transformations' is the overarching word for all movements of a shape in a plane. Reflections, rotations and translations are all types of transformations that keep the size and shape exactly the same. Enlargements are also transformations but they change the size of the shape.

The language of reflections can be confusing and it is important to emphasise that a reflection *'in'* the mirror keeps every point of the image at an equal distance from the mirror to the corresponding point of the object.

Key questions to develop understanding

- What angle have you turned through?
- How far is that point from the mirror?
- Can you describe the translation precisely?

Follow up activities

1. Investigate the effect of combining two transformations, for example two reflections in different mirror lines. Start with two mirror lines parallel to each other. In this case the combined transformation will be a translation. What will be the direction of the translation and how far will the image be from the object?

2. What will the effect be of two rotations:
   - with the same center of rotation?
   - with different centers of rotation?

3. Interesting and creative patterns can be made by tessellating shapes based on a triangle or a parallelogram. Cut out part of the shape and attach that part to a parallel edge. The new shape will tessellate to create a different pattern. You can find more ideas and information on these sites:

   Tessellating triangles http://nrich.maths.org/98
   Tessellating quadrilaterals http://nrich.maths.org/11505
   Maurits Cornelius Escher http://nrich.maths.org/2578

4. On squared paper draw axes from –4 to 4 for x and y. Draw a stick figure with the top of its head at (1.5, 3). Write down the coordinates of the feet and the body.

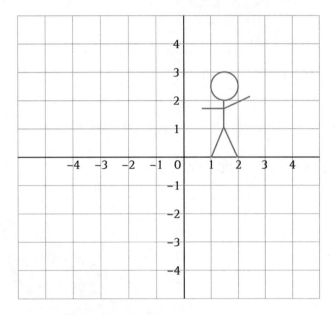

Transform each coordinate by $(x, y) \rightarrow (x + 2, y + 1)$.

Draw the pin figure with the new coordinates. Describe the transformation.

Now try $(x, y) \rightarrow (-x, -y)$ (starting from the original stick figure).

What would you need to do to the coordinates to reflect the figure in the y-axis?

What else can you make the figure do by changing the coordinates? Can you make it jump higher? Can you make it lie down?

Image of the quadrilateral after translation and rotation

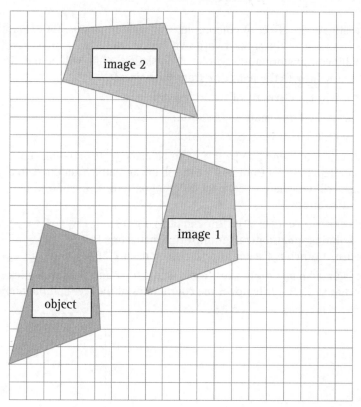

Reflecting a triangle in its long side.

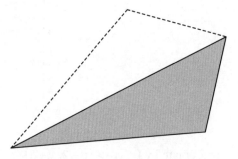

Rotating a quadrilateral by a half-turn about the middle of one edge.

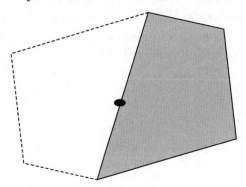

Area and perimeter

Teaching strategy: Visual and practical

Curriculum content

Area and perimeter of 2D shapes, effect of doubling length on area

Prior knowledge needed

Understanding of concept of area and perimeter

Intended Learning Outcomes

At the end of this activity teachers and learners will:

- Know that if two shapes have the same area they don't necessarily have the same perimeter and vice versa
- Understand the effect that doubling the perimeter has on the area of a shape
- Be able to calculate the area and perimeter of a circle
- Appreciate that there is a relationship between the radius and the area and perimeter of a circle
- Have experienced measuring perimeter and area using centimetres and square centimetres

Fact box

The perimeter of a shape is the distance around the edge of the shape and is measured in length units, e.g. mm, cm, m.

Perimeter of a circle $= 2\pi r$

The area of a shape is the space that the shape covers and is measured in square units, e.g. mm^2, cm^2, m^2.

Area of a triangle $= \frac{1}{2}$ base × perpendicular height

Area of parallelogram $=$ base × perpendicular height

Area of a circle $= \pi r^2$

Resources for this workshop
Centimetre square paper page 199; string; compasses; scissors; photocopy of page 194.

Workshop Activities for Teachers

Activity 1: Same perimeter different area, same area different perimeter

> • Centimetre square paper (page **199**)
>
> *Pairs, whole group*   *30 minutes*

Same perimeter

Work in pairs. Each person gets a sheet of centimetre square paper and draws four different shapes which all have a **perimeter** of 20 cm. Write the perimeter outside each shape. Now swop your piece of paper with your partner. Work out the **area** of each of the four shapes. Write the **area** inside the shape.

What do you notice?

Same area

Work with the same partner. Each take a new piece of centimetre square paper. This time draw four shapes which all have an **area** of 12 square centimetres. Write the area inside each shape. Swop your pieces of paper and work out the **perimeter** of each of your partner's shapes. Write the **perimeter** on the outside of the shape.

What do you notice?

> **Notes**
> See the learner activity for an example of a shape with perimeter 20 cm and a shape with area 12 square centimetres. You should notice that shapes with the same perimeter **do not** always have the same area and that shapes with the same area **do not** always have the same perimeter.
>
> If you can't photocopy the centimetre square paper use lined paper and draw in vertical lines to make a grid of squares.

Activity 2: Twice as big

> • Centimetre square paper (page **199**)
>
> *Pairs, whole group*   *20 minutes*

Work in pairs. Each person gets a sheet of centimetre square paper and draws a rectangle. Write the perimeter of the rectangle on the outside and the area of the rectangle (in a different colour) on the inside. Swop your pieces of paper.

On your partner's piece of paper, draw a new rectangle that has a length and breadth that is twice as long as the first rectangle. Write the perimeter of the rectangle on the outside and the area of the rectangle (in a different colour) on the inside.

What do you notice about the relationship between the old perimeter and the new perimeter and between the old area and the new area?

Repeat the activity but draw a different polygon. See below for some ideas:

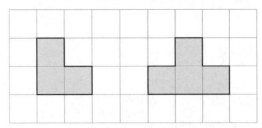

> **Notes**
> You should notice that if the perimeter of a shape doubles (becomes twice as big), the area becomes four times bigger. When doing this activity with learners it is important to use a variety of different shapes and not only rectangles. Learners need to be able to see that this works for any shape.
>
> To say a shape is twice as big is not clear. You need to say whether the perimeter is twice as big OR the area is twice as big.

Activity 3: Perimeter of circle

> • String; compasses
>
> *Pairs, whole group*   *20 minutes*

Work through classroom activity 2.

Each pair can draw three circles (with diameter 12 cm, 15 cm and 20 cm).

Work as accurately as you can.

Discuss as a group whether this activity will work in your class.

How can you adapt it to a whole class activity if you don't have enough compasses or scissors for learners to work in pairs? Think about ways in which you can still engage all the learners. Share ways in which you help your learners remember the difference between the formula for the circumference of a circle and the area of a circle.

> **Notes**
> The perimeter of a circle is $2\pi r$ the area of a circle is πr^2. The π symbol can seem strange to learners but it is just a number. It may be easier to see which formula is a length and which an area if you write 3.14 as an approximation for π. The formula $2 \times 3.14 \times r$ is just a number times a length so this is the perimeter. $3.14 \times r^2 = 3.14 \times r \times r$ has the length r multiplied by the length r so this is an area.
>
> If you have time look at ways to visualise the formulae for the area of a triangle, a parallelogram and a circle on page 131.

Classroom Activities for Learners

Activity 1: Twice as big

> • Centimetre square paper
>
> *Pairs, whole group*   *45 minutes*

Draw a square grid on the board. It should be at least 12 by 6.

Draw a 2 × 3 rectangle on the grid. Mark the bottom left-hand corner with a dot.

Choose a point on the grid to the right of the rectangle and tell the class that they must help you draw a rectangle with sides twice as long as the first one.

Indicate that you moved up 2 units from your reference point on your original rectangle. Ask your learners how far you will move up from your new reference point if you are drawing a rectangle twice as big. You can start drawing a vertical line up and they should tell you when to stop.

On the original rectangle you then moved right by 3 units. Ask the learners by how many units you will move right in your new rectangle. Or start moving right and they must tell you when to stop.

Write the perimeter of each rectangle on the outside and the area on the inside.

When you are finished you should have the following on the board:

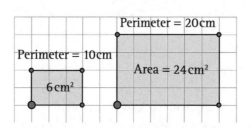 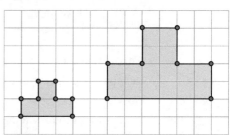

Repeat the activity using a different polygon.

Divide your class into pairs. Give each learner a sheet of centimetre square paper and tell them to draw a rectangle. They should write the perimeter on the outside and the area (in a different colour) on the inside. Tell the learners to swop their pieces of paper with their partner. They must now draw a new rectangle with sides twice as long as the one their partner drew. And then they must also write the perimeter on the outside and the area (in a different colour) on the inside.

Ask the class what they notice about the relationship between the old perimeter and the new perimeter and between the old area and the new area.

> **Teaching ideas**
> • As much as possible you want your learners to see the relationship themselves. Draw two columns on the board. *Area of starting shape and Area of shape with sides twice as long*. Let each pair fill in their areas on the board. It is much easier to see a pattern when you have lots of examples.
> • Encourage them to write down in words what they notice: the perimeter is twice as long and the area is four times as big.
> • Some of them might struggle with enlarging a shape by a factor of two so spend enough time at the beginning explaining how each length is doubled.
> • This activity is also an opportunity to emphasise the concepts of area and perimeter – that perimeter has to do with length around the edge of an object and area has to do with space covered.

Activity 2: Circumference of circle

- Long piece of string for each pair (around 1.5 m); compasses

Pairs, whole group   *45 minutes*

Measuring the circumference

Divide the class up into pairs. Give each group a piece of string 1.5 m long. Here are the instructions for your learners:

1. Use a compass to draw a circle with a diameter of either 12 cm, 15 cm or 20 cm. *Make sure that there is at least one group that has chosen each of the three diameters.*

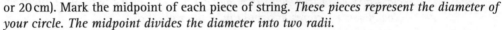

2. Use the string to measure the **circumference** of your circle. Cut the piece of string so that it is as long as the circumference.

3. Cut the rest of your string into pieces that are as long as the diameter of your circle (12 cm, 15 cm or 20 cm). Mark the midpoint of each piece of string. *These pieces represent the diameter of your circle. The midpoint divides the diameter into two radii.*

4. Lay the piece of string that is as long as the circumference of your circle straight on the desk. Now use the diameter pieces to see approximately how many diameters you need to make the circumference.

Questions to ask the learners

1. If you have a circle with a diameter of 40 cm, approximately how long will the circumference be?

2. Measure a piece of string with this length and use it to make a circle. Does your circle have a diameter of 40 cm?

Teaching ideas

- The main aim of this activity is that the learners appreciate that there is a **constant** relationship between the diameter (and also the radius) of a circle and its circumference. It is therefore important that you point out to the class that even though different pairs had different circles, everyone found the same relationship between the diameter and the circumference. Because of this constant relationship we can work out the circumference if we know only the diameter (or radius). The approximate relationship is that the circumference is 3 times the diameter. The exact relationship is that the circumference is pi times the diameter. In other words:

  Circumference of circle = π × diameter.

- Because the diameter is 2 times the radius we often write this as:

  Circumference of circle = π × 2 × radius = $2\pi r$.

- If your learners already know the formula for the circumference of a circle, this activity will emphasise that π is a number with a value close to 3.

Changes to my classroom practice

Implementing the teaching strategy

Visual and practical learning styles   *see page 4*

Although learners must be able to use mathematical notation to write down things like the formula for the area of a circle, it is important that when they are first introduced to a new concept they see it in a visual way.

When learners try to double all the sides of a shape they first need to **see** how the sides fit together to make up the shape.

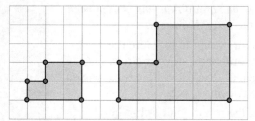

Ask a learner to come to the board and describe precisely how to draw the small L-shape.

e.g. Mark a starting point then move 1 square vertically to make the first side.
Now move 1 squares horizontally to the right, etc.

Ask the learner to repeat the instructions but this time to double all the lengths.
e.g. Mark a starting point then move 2 squares vertically
Draw exactly what the learner says, without comment, even when they make a mistake. The class will soon notice if something is wrong!

New concepts can be linked to prior knowledge so that learners can make connections to what they already know. For example the knowledge of the area of a rectangle is used to find the area of a parallelogram. This gives a visual way of understanding where the formula comes from and why it is the perpendicular height in the formula and ***not*** the sloping side.

Key questions to develop understanding

- What stays the same and what is different?
- Does the area stay the same when you keep the perimeter the same?
- Does the perimeter stay the same when you keep the area the same?
- How does the area of the shape change when you double all the lengths of the shape?
- How would the area change if you tripled all the lengths of the sides?
- For each circle you need approximately the same number of diameters to get the perimeter. Approximately how many diameters do you need?
- What would the perimeter be if the diameter was 4 m? Or 17 m? Or 125 m?

Follow up activities

In Classroom Activity 2 you saw an example of how to visualise the formula for the circumference of a circle. Below are ideas for additional activities to visualise the formula for the area of a triangle, the area of a parallelogram and the area of a circle.

Area of a triangle

Draw a triangle on a piece of paper. Choose one side to be the base. Cut the triangle out and use it to draw another identical triangle. Cut out the second triangle. If you can, make each triangle a different colour. Now draw the perpendicular height on the second triangle. Label the height on the triangle. Cut along this height. You now have three pieces. Can you arrange these three pieces into a rectangle? What is the area of the rectangle in terms of the base of the triangle and its perpendicular height?

If the area of two triangles equals base × perpendicular height, what will the area of one triangle equal?

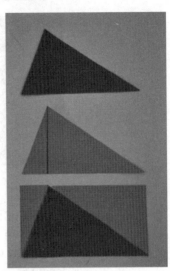

Area of a parallelogram

Draw a parallelogram on squared paper and cut it out.

Can you see how to cut the parallelogram into two pieces which fit together to make a rectangle.

How can you use this to explain the formula for the area of a parallelogram to your class?

Discuss the important similarities and difference between the formula for the area of a rectangle and the formula for the area of a parallelogram.

The cut must be perpendicular to the base to make a rectangle. That explains why the formula for the area of a parallelogram needs the **perpendicular** height.

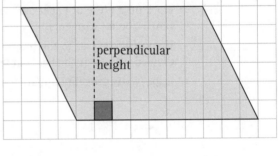

Area of circle

Make two copies of the circle on page **194**. Keep the one as it is. Cut the other one up into 12 segments. Cut the 12th segment into two smaller segments. Now arrange the 13 segments as indicated below.

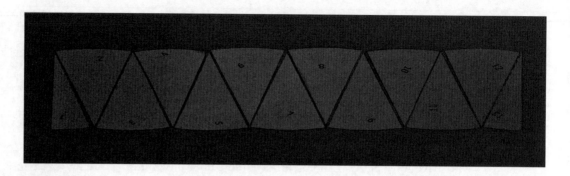

You now have a shape that is approximately a rectangle. The area of this shape is the same as the area of the circle as they are made from the same segments. Work out a formula for the area of this approximate rectangle.

The length of the rectangle is half of the perimeter of the circle so

length $= \frac{1}{2} \times$ perimeter $= \frac{1}{2} \times 2\pi r = \pi r$. The breadth of the rectangle is the radius of the circle so breadth $= r$. So the area of the rectangle $=$ length $\times$ breadth $= \pi r \times r = \pi r^2$.

If you can't make photocopies you can use a wall clock to make the circles. Place the wall clock on a piece of paper and draw around it. Make a mark at each hour to divide the circle into 12 equal segments.

If you have access to the Internet you can use the following applet to see how the circle can be divided into even smaller segments so that you can approximate the area even better:

http://www.geogebra.org/student/m279

Teaching strategy: Visual and practical

Curriculum content

Compare the properties of 3-dimensional (3D) objects, including the numbers of faces, edges and vertices. Identify polyhedra, including the Platonic solids.

Prior knowledge needed

Properties and names of 2-dimensional (2D) shapes.

Intended Learning Outcomes

At the end of this activity teachers and learners will:

- Know the names and properties of some common 3D objects
- Understand how to interpret nets and sketches and use them in making geometrical models
- Be able to discuss the properties of prisms, pyramids and Platonic solids
- Appreciate some of the symmetries, patterns and properties of Platonic solids
- Have experienced the confidence created by collaborative practical work

Fact box

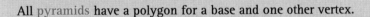

Face: a flat surface
Edge: a line along which two faces meet
Vertex: a point where edges and faces meet

A 3-dimensional solid is a polyhedron if its faces are polygons. e.g. the faces of a triangular prism are rectangles and triangles so it is a polyhedron.

A cylinder is a solid but not a polyhedron.

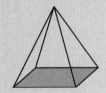

Cylinder

All pyramids have a polygon for a base and one other vertex.

A square-based pyramid has a square base and all the corners (vertices) of the base are joined to the vertex at the top.

Square-based pyramid

All prisms have two parallel polygonal faces joined by parallel lines.

A triangular prism has two parallel triangular faces joined by parallel lines.

Triangular prism

Regular solids (also called Platonic solids) must have all the edge lengths the same and all the angles equal. All the faces of a regular polyhedron are congruent regular polygons. For example, a cube is a regular polyhedron. A triangular prism is a polyhedron but it is not regular.

Resources for this workshop
*Sticky tape; string and scissors; used A4 paper or magazines, so each teacher can make at least 6 rolled paper sticks. **See page 138 now** for how to make the sticks. If possible make some of the sticks **BEFORE** the workshop. Photocopy of pages 140, 195 and 196.*

Workshop Activities for Teachers

Activity 1: Puzzles with rolled paper sticks

- Used A4 paper or magazine paper to make at least 90 rolled paper sticks, all the same length

Pairs and then whole group   *45 minutes if the sticks are made in advance*

Follow the instructions on page **138** to make the rolled paper sticks.

Four triangles puzzle

Working in pairs, tie 5 sticks of the same length together to make two triangles as shown. Lay them flat on the table.

Add a 6th stick of the same length to the two triangles to make four triangles.

 Try this now

What shape have you made? What can you say about it?

Making the icosahedron

 Try this now

Make 6 rhombuses as shown out of 3 colours, with 5 sticks for each one.

Tie the rhombuses together to make this pattern noting how the different coloured rhombuses fit into the pattern. Tie the shapes together to make an icosahedron with 20 triangular faces.

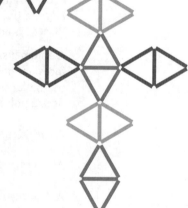

At times it may seem impossible that the floppy sticks will ever join to make a solid shape. You will succeed if you keep checking that you have 5 sticks at every vertex and that each face is a triangle. See photos on page **139**.

What properties of the icosahedron do you notice?

Discussion of planning for practical activities

Read through Classroom Activity 1 and discuss how you will plan for this practical activity. Can you arrange for the sticks to be made before the lesson so that you will have time for the icosahedron activity or will you get the paper and string together so that the learners make the sticks in the lesson? This organisation of resources is crucial to the success of a practical lesson.

Notes
- This activity naturally takes you from flat shapes in 2 dimensions (2D) to solid shapes in 3 dimensions (3D). Talk about what is meant by 'dimensions'.
- The shape with four triangular faces is a triangle-based **pyramid** with the special name **tetrahedron**. A shape is **regular** if all the edge lengths and all the angles are equal so your tetrahedron is a regular solid. Look at the **icosahedron** that you have made. Check that it is also regular.

Activity 2: Nets of 3D objects

* Scissors; sticky tape
* Photocopy of net puzzle on page **140** and photocopy of net of octahedron on page **195**

Pairs then whole group   *45 minutes*

1. Check the fact box to make sure that you know the difference between a pyramid and a prism. Now use your photocopy to try the net puzzle on page **140**.
2. **Octahedron.** Use the net on page **195** to make an octahedron.
3. Make a collection of all your models. Then each person in the group should say something about the properties of the models.

Activity 3: Platonic solids

* Collection of the models you have made
* Photocopy of net of dodecahedron on page **196**

Groups of 3 or 4   *45 minutes*

1. From all the solids you have made pick the **regular** ones where all the faces are equilateral triangles. Put them in order according to the number of triangles at each vertex: 3, 4 or 5. Is it possible to make a regular solid with 6 or 7 equilateral triangles at each vertex?

2. How many regular polyhedra do you know with squares as faces?

   How many squares meet at each vertex?

   Is it possible to make a solid with 4 squares meeting together at a vertex?

3. What about a regular polyhedron with pentagonal faces? This is a solid with three pentagons at each vertex. It is called a **dodecahedron**. To complete your collection of platonic solids use the net on page **196** to make a dodecahedron. Could you have 4 pentagons at each vertex?

4. What about hexagonal faces? Could you make a solid with hexagonal faces?

   Why or why not?

Notes
* If you don't have a cube in your collection copy this net onto squared paper to make one. Looking at the net will also help you to see how the squares fold up to meet at each vertex.

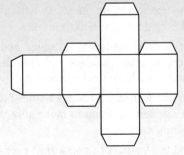

* There are only five Platonic solids: three made of triangles (tetrahedron, octahedron and icosahedron), one made of squares (cube) and one made of pentagons (dodecahedron). No other regular polyhedra are possible.

Classroom Activities for Learners

Activity 1: Polyhedron puzzles

- Rolled paper sticks

Pairs then whole group   *50 minutes*

Making the rolled paper sticks

If possible organise the making of rolled paper sticks, all the same length, ahead of the lesson. Allow at least 6 sticks for each learner.

A puzzle

Working in pairs, tie 5 sticks of the same length together to make two triangles as shown.

Lay them flat on the table.

Join a 6th stick of the same length to the two triangles to make four triangles.

Discussion of properties

Tell the learners that the shape they have made is called a tetrahedron.

Introduce or review edges, faces and vertices.

Icosahedron puzzle

If the rolled paper sticks have been made before the lesson the class may have time to work in groups to make the icosahedron as described in the teacher activities.

Octahedron puzzle

If you have fewer sticks and less time the learners can try this puzzle to turn the square made of 12 sticks into a solid octahedron.

An octahedron has 8 triangular faces.

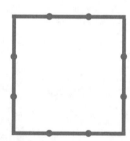

Teaching ideas

- Tell the learners to tie the sticks with a bow that is easy to undo as they might make mistakes and need to make changes.

- Whilst learners are busily occupied and discussing the activity, teachers have time to listen, observe and assist individuals. By asking probing questions they can encourage mathematical reasoning.

- An icosahedron has 30 edges with 5 faces at each vertex. Watch what the learners are doing. Remind them to make sure they join just 5 edges at each vertex with one stick along each edge.

- Remind the learners to check that every face is a triangle.

- Ask learners to count the number of vertices, edges and faces.

- Ask learners what they notice about the pattern of colours in the icosahedron they have made.

- Wire or drinking straws can be used for these puzzles but rolled paper sticks are easier to link together.

Activity 2: Nets of prisms and pyramids

- Collection of shapes; showboards
- Photocopy of net puzzle on page **140** for each pair

Whole group, pairs   *50 minutes*

Preparation before the lesson

You will need: scissors, sticky tape, a tetrahedron made from rolled paper sticks and a square-based pyramid. Bring in several cardboard boxes to demonstrate rectangular prisms and (if possible) a triangular prism. Photocopy the net puzzle on page **140**.

Class discussion: naming of pyramids and prisms

Hold up shapes and ask your learners to talk about the shapes, to name them and to count the edges, vertices and faces.

Showboards are useful for getting replies, or ask learners to show the number by holding up their fingers.

Explain how to identify a square-based pyramid from its square base and a triangle-based pyramid from its triangular base.

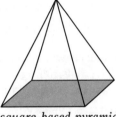
square-based pyramid

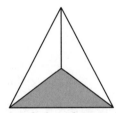
triangle-based pyramid also called a tetrahedron

Talk about how, for all pyramids, all the vertices of the base are joined to a single point (vertex) at the top.

All prisms have some rectangular faces. Boxes are often rectangular prisms and you get a rectangle wherever you cut parallel to any face.

For triangular prisms you get a triangle if you cut parallel to the triangular faces.

Hold up a variety of shapes and ask the class if they are prisms or pyramids...then ask **why**?

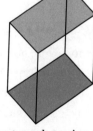
rectangular prism

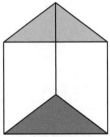
triangular prism

Making solids from nets

Give each pair a photocopy of the net puzzle on page **140**. They need to find the two pieces that will make a solid, to cut them out and to use sticky tape to put them together.

> **Teaching ideas**
> - If you don't have a model of a triangular prism fold a sheet of paper into three parts to make a triangular prism open at both ends.
> - An informal way to remember the names is that prisms are good for making sandwiches, wherever you cut you get the same cross-section.

Changes in my classroom practice

Implementing the teaching strategy

| *Visual and practical learning styles* | *see page 4* |

It is important for learners to see and handle solid shapes for themselves because pictures in a book or diagrams on the chalkboard can be meaningless without the practical experience. When the class has made the models they might be hung up from the ceiling of the classroom. Repeated reference to the names of the shapes and to their properties will help the learners to visualise and to remember them.

- The rolled paper stick models help learners to count the numbers of edges and vertices. The sticks make the edges and the points where the sticks are tied together make the vertices of your solids
- The nets help learners to count the number of faces of the solids.
- Trying to draw 3D shapes (see page **198**) will help the learners interpret the diagrams.

A variety of models will help learners to visualise 3D shapes so you need to organise the materials. If you have storage space then build up a collection of models and containers. Encourage learners to bring in a variety of cardboard packages.

Games and puzzles enhance lessons as long as the learning objective is clear because, even if solving the puzzles takes time, teachers often find that learners enjoy the activities so much that they learn and remember more than usual. The learning objective here is to become familiar with some of the common polyhedra so the puzzles are only a means to an end, not an end in themselves. The puzzles can be fun to solve again and again because it is not easy to remember what to do. Letting learners play with them out of lesson time will re-enforce the learning.

Key questions to develop understanding

Answer the following questions about each of the polyhedra:

- What can you tell me about the shape we've made?
- How many edges has the shape got?
- How many vertices has the shape got?
- How many faces has the shape got?
- What symmetry can you see in the shape?

Making resources

How to make rolled paper sticks

You need: Sticky tape, string, used A4 paper or magazine pages all cut to the same size.

1. Cut a piece of string long enough to overlap paper at both sides. Stick string to short edge of paper with sticky tape so that it does not slip out of the roll.
2. Roll up **very tightly** and secure with more sticky tape.

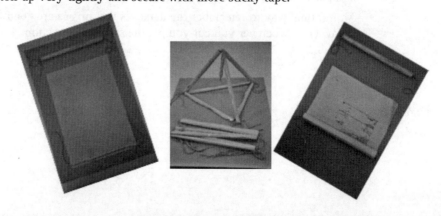

Additional activity

More tetrahedron puzzles

Draw the 5 patterns shown on the board.

Each pair of learners should choose one of the patterns, make a copy of their chosen pattern by tying 6 sticks together and then make this into a regular tetrahedron.

	Number of faces	Number of edges	Number of vertices
Triangular Faces			
TETRAHEDRON			
OCTAHEDRON			
ICOSAHEDRON	20	30	12
Square Faces			
CUBE			
Pentagonal Faces			
DODECAHEDRON	12	30	20

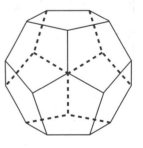

Dodecahedron

Can you complete this table now?

Net puzzle

Cut out these four shapes. Make two solid
shapes one with 4 vertices and one with
5 vertices. Use sticky tape to fix them together.
What are the names of your shapes?

Surface area and volume

Teaching strategy: Visual and practical

Curriculum content

Familiarity with 3D models and diagrams needed to successfully use formulae and units to calculate surface area and volume

Prior knowledge needed

Area of rectangle and triangle, linear measures, net of cube

Intended Learning Outcomes

At the end of this activity teachers and learners will:

• Know measurements needed to find surface area and volume of cubes and triangular prisms
• Understand how to calculate surface area and volume of cubes and prisms
• Be able to visualise the net of simple solids and interpret 3D diagrams
• Appreciate that volume is measured by packing unit cubes into a solid
• Have experienced working with solids and nets of solids

Fact box

Units

If lengths of the sides of a shape are in cm then the unit of measurement of area is a 1 cm by 1 cm square. This is $1\,cm^2$.

If lengths of the sides of a shape are in cm then unit of measurement of volume is a 1 cm by 1 cm by 1 cm cube. This is $1\,cm^3$.

Surface area of a cube

A cube with sides of 3 cm has 6 square faces each measuring 3 cm by 3 cm.

So **surface area of a cube of side 3 cm is $6 \times 3 \times 3\,cm^2$.**

Volume of a cube

A cube of side 3 cm can fit $3 \times 3 = 9$ unit cubes in the base layer.

Three layers will fill the cube so the **volume of a cube with side 3 cm is $3 \times 3 \times 3 = 27\,cm^3$.**

In general, a cube of side a has a surface area of $6a^2$ and a volume a^3.

A rectangular prism with base a rectangle W × B and length L has

    Surface area 2WB + 2WL+ 2BL and

    Volume W × B × L which can also be written Base Area × Length

Resources for this workshop

Each pair needs two cardboard boxes (e.g. toothpaste or tea packet); squared paper; scissors; sticky tape; coloured marker pens and compasses. A4 paper, wooden or plastic cubes if available or use cubes made during the workshop from paper.

Workshop Activities for Teachers

Activity 1: Visualising surface area

- Each pair **must have** two cardboard boxes
- Squared paper; coloured marker pens; scissors; sticky tape; compasses

Pair, individual, whole group   *60 minutes*

Surface area

Read through Classroom Activity 1: Surface area of cardboard boxes on page **144**. Cover one cardboard box with squared paper and mark it to show the formula for calculating the surface area of a rectangular prism.

Making cubes

Work individually (but talk to your partner about the shapes as you work) and draw the net of a cube of side 3 cm on square dotty paper. Fold up and stick with sticky tape. Calculate the surface area. Make a second cube exactly the same size as this will be needed later.

Cutting open a cardboard box to show the net

Take another cardboard box. Stick down any open flaps. Then use scissors to cut round 3 sides and open up a lid. Make more cuts until you have a flat net of your box.

Making a rectangular prism

On square dotty paper draw the net of a rectangular prism with length 10 cm, width 5 cm and height 3 cm. Before you fold up the rectangular prism mark all the 10 cm lengths in one colour and use two other colours for the 5 cm sides and the 3 cm sides. Calculate the area of each face and mark it clearly in the centre.

Choose one person to be the teacher. They should explain what surface area means, get the group to calculate the surface area of the cubes and prisms they have made and work out a formula for the surface area of a rectangular prism of length L, width W and height H by finding the area of each side and writing it on the model.

In your group discuss the following three approaches you could take to teaching surface area. Try to think of at least one advantage, and one disadvantage for each method.

- **Using solid shapes:** This approach looks at the areas of the surfaces on the solid shape and involves measuring lengths.
- **Using nets:** This approach requires learners to works with the nets of a cube and a rectangular prism.
- **Starting with a formula:** In this approach the teacher writes the formula on the board, draws a diagram, gets the learners to copy it down and to start exercises straight away.

Work with someone who likes the same method as you to discuss how you will teach and how you will extend your preferred method to the surface area of a triangular prism.

Get a volunteer to demonstrate their method for a triangular prism.

Notes

Whatever approach you prefer, a collection of cardboard boxes is an excellent resource. Bring in a few examples several weeks before teaching the topic and ask learners to contribute at least one box to the collection. It is possible to find packages that are triangular prisms and these are especially useful.

Activity 2: Visualising on a grand scale!

- Cubes made of paper, wood or plastic

Pairs, whole group *40 minutes*

Packing cubes

Try Classroom Activity 2 on packing cubes in layers. Use the paper cubes you made in Activity 1 to show how the layers build up.

Shut your eyes

Now try this visualisation exercise. Get someone to act as the teacher reading it out very slowly to the whole group so you can shut your eyes and concentrate.

- Imagine you have a large packing case measuring 1 metre × 1 metre × 1 metre and lots and lots of cubes measuring 1 cm × 1 cm × 1 cm.
- You fit the 1 cm × 1 cm × 1 cm cubes carefully in a line across the base of the packing case.
- Then you add lots more lines of cubes until the base of the packing case is completely covered.
- This has taken ages so you take a break. When you come back your irritating younger brother has taken all the cubes out and used them to build a tower placing one cube above another and sticking them with glue. Will the tower reach the ceiling?

Open your eyes and work out how high the tower is.

Shut your eyes again so the teacher can continue.

- That was just one layer of cubes.
- Now imagine adding more and more layers until the box is full.
- If the cubes are taken out and made into a tower how high would it be?
- Would it be as high as Table Mountain*?

Open your eyes and do the calculation.

> **Notes**
> - A tower from just the base layer of cubes is 100 cm × 100 cm = 10 000 cm = 100 m. It won't just reach the ceiling it would reach the top of …. Insert local hill or tower or something the learners in your class will be familiar with.
> - *Use a mountain your learners would have heard about. Table Mountain is 1085 m high, Mount Kilimanjaro is 5895 m and Mount Everest is 8 848 metre high. The tower is 100 × 100 × 100 cm high. That is 1 000 000 cm.

Classroom Activities for Learners

Activity 1: Surface area of cardboard boxes

- Collection of cardboard packaging, scissors, squared paper, glue or sticky tape
- Showboards

Fours, whole group 50 minutes

Looking at a collection of boxes. Hold up a variety of cardboard packages, e.g. packets for tea or detergent.

Ask the learners to count the faces and hold up fingers (or use showboards) to show the number of faces. For cubes and rectangular prisms this will always be six faces. Are the shapes of the faces squares or rectangles? Do any of the packets have triangular faces? Other shapes?

Covering the boxes. Each group of four has the task of completely covering their rectangular prism with squared paper. They must work out what measurements they need to make on the box and the size of each sheet to be cut out.

Recording. Each learner should make a record of their work. For example:

The longest side of our rectangular prism was 12 cm.

The base of our prism measured 9 cm × 6 cm.

We cut out rectangles measuring ... So total surface srea was ...

Demonstration to whole class. Take a large rectangular prism (e.g. box for photocopy paper) and with a marker pen colour the length red and mark it L.

Ask a learner to the front to find a length exactly the same and colour it.

Repeat for height H.

How would we find the area of this base? ... Multiply H × W. Write H × W large in centre of the side.

Continue until the area of each side is marked. Show them the formula in their textbooks and set examples.

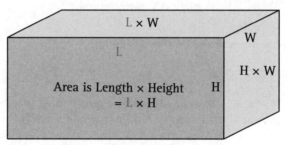

Continue until every face of the box is labelled.

Teaching ideas

It is crucial to collect enough cardboard boxes in advance for this lesson. A large demonstration box for the teacher and coloured marker pens will give the lesson more impact. The demonstration box can stay in the classroom for a week or two as a reminder.

Activity 2: Finding volume by packing cubes in layers

- Cubes, one large box

Pairs, whole group *50 minutes*

Remind the class that you measure area by finding how many unit squares will pack into a shape.

So what about volume? Discuss what volume means and how we measure it with cubes.

Hold up a large rectangular prism. Tell the learners: "By the end of this lesson I expect you to be able to calculate the volume **and** explain why you are right."

So start with something simpler a 3 × 3 × 3 cm cube.

Draw a 3 cm × 3 cm square in your books. This is the base of the cube. I want you to imagine packing 1 cm cubes into your base. Work in pairs you have 1 minute to decide how many cubes you could pack on your base. Show me with your fingers. *9 cubes.*

Now shut your eyes and imagine putting another layer of cubes on top of your base layer. Does that make a 3 cm high cube? Work with a partner to decide how many layers and how many cubes altogether.

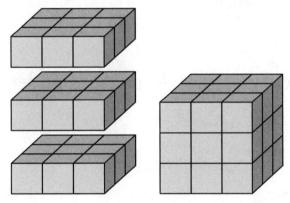

Teaching ideas

This activity is a lot easier if you have a supply of cubes: wooden cubes, cubes the learners have made from paper or card, plastic (multilink) cubes. You can demonstrate the idea of layers with larger cubes. If you don't have cubes photocopy the image on page 147.

Changes in my classroom practice

Implementing the teaching strategy

Visual and Practical learning styles   *see page 4*

Practical activities

List the skills the learners use in covering a box with squared paper and calculating the surface area in a practical way. How will you use this to help learners when they are working on textbook problems on surface area or volume?

Visualisation

Providing pictures and objects for learners to look at is the obvious way of helping learners to visualise but we are all also capable of making images in our heads. Many learners will be able to describe exactly how a goal was scored at a football match or how a runner won a race. You can capture this ability by asking the learners to shut their eyes and think about mathematical shapes.

Key questions to develop understanding

Surface Area

- How many faces?
- Are any faces exactly the same size?

Volume

- How many cubes will fit in the base layer?
- How many layers fit in the box?

Follow up activity

Finding the volume of a triangular prism

This is a triangular prism. The base is a right-angled triangle. The two short sides measure 3 cm and 4 cm. The length is 8 cm.

Photocopy or copy the net on page **148**.

Cut out two nets for your prism and fit them together to make a rectangular prism.

What is the volume of the rectangular prism?

So what is the volume of the two triangular prisms?

Explain how this links to this formula:

Volume of triangular prism = Area of base × Length of prism.

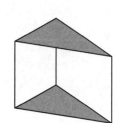

Errors and misconceptions

A common error is not understanding that 2HL means 2 × H × L.

All the activities in this chapter are designed to help the learner **see** that these are not just meaningless letters but a description of part of the surface area of a rectangular prism.

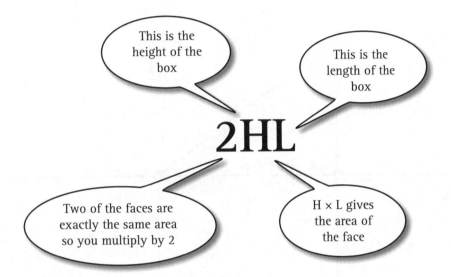

The volume of a cube of side *a* is a^3. A common misconception is that this means *a* is multiplied by 3.

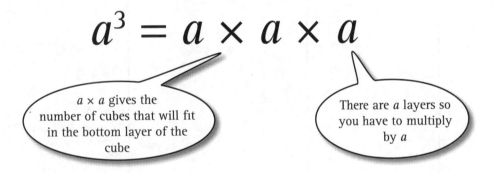

Image for volume of cube

Each small cube measures 1 cm × 1 cm × 1 cm. What is the volume of the cube?

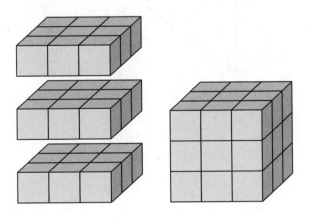

Net of a triangular prism

Use this net to make two triangular prisms exactly the same size. Fit the triangular prisms together to make a rectangular prism.

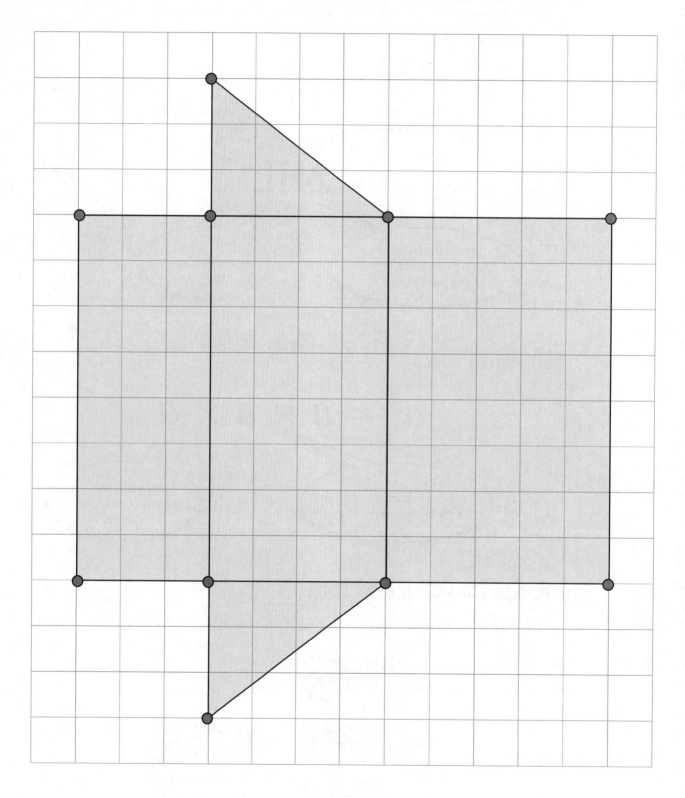

Provoking discussion of probability

Teaching strategy: Discussion

Curriculum content

Language of probability, calculating theoretical probability

Prior knowledge needed

Ideas of chance. Equivalent fractions.

Intended Learning Outcomes

At the end of this activity teachers and learners will:

- Know how theoretical probability is defined and calculated
- Understand when the probability of an event can be estimated by an experiment or by considering available evidence
- Be able to calculate the theoretical probability in a variety of situations
- Appreciate the value of activities which involve learners in discussion of probability concepts
- Have experienced using the formal language of probability to explain their ideas

Fact box

Probability is a way to express mathematically the chance that an event occurs.

The probability of an event is a number between 0 (impossible) and 1 (certain to happen).

The possible outcomes of an event are all the things that can happen.
e.g. When you toss a coin there are two possible outcomes: heads or tails.

Sometimes we can work out a theoretical probability. For us to be able to do this we need to know all possible outcomes and be sure that the outcomes are all equally likely.
e.g. What is the probability of getting an even number when we throw a dice?

There are 6 possible outcomes: 1, 2, 3, 4, 5, 6. If the dice is fair they are all equally likely.

Getting an even number 2, 4, 6 is called a successful outcome.

$$\text{Probability of an even number} = \frac{\text{Number of successful outcomes}}{\text{Number of equally likely possible outcomes}}$$
$$= \frac{3}{6} = \frac{1}{2}$$

Sometimes we can work out the experimental probability of an event either by carrying out a large number of trials or by using data gathered in the past.

What is the probability that Manchester United will beat the school football team? There are 3 possible outcomes Win, Lose, Draw but because they are not equally likely we cannot find a theoretical probability. Looking at all the matches played by both teams it seems likely that the school team would lose!

Resources for this workshop
Card; string; pegs; paper. Photocopy page 156 for each teacher.

Workshop Activities for Teachers

Activity 1: What's the chance of these events?

> - Card; string; pegs
> *Pairs, whole group*   *40 minutes*

From impossible to certain

Write each of these events on a separate strip of paper:

1. I will throw a dice and get a four.
2. Our teacher will set Maths homework today.
3. If Manchester United played the school football team our team would win.
4. I will toss a coin and get heads.
5. There are 4 red balls and one blue ball in a bag. Without looking I take a ball and get a blue ball.
6. It will rain tomorrow.

Work in pairs and put the events in order from impossible to certain. Which events can you be sure of the probability? Which events are you estimating a probability based on past experience?

Probability washing line

Stretch a piece of string across the front of the room or, if you have no string, draw a line on the board. Write impossible at one end, certain at the other. Impossible, no chance is represented by 0. Absolutely certain is represented by 1. So a fifty-fifty chance would be in the middle of the line.

Each pair should peg the cards to the line and explain why they have decided on this order and this position on the line. The purpose of this workshop is to encourage talking about probability.

When you have argued and agreed about the order, try inventing your own probability events that you think would interest your learners. You need a mix of events where you can find the theoretical probability and events where you have experimental evidence of what might happen.

> **Notes**
> - Learners already know that:
>   - some things are much more likely to occur than others.
>   - when you toss a coin you have an even (50–50 chance) of getting a head.
> - In everyday language we use a range of words from impossible, very unlikely, unlikely, even chance, likely, very likely, certain to describe what we think will happen.
> - After discussion you want learners to appreciate that:
>   - A scale is used to describe probability with 0 an impossible event and 1 for a certain event.
>   - You can calculate a theoretical probability if you can list all the events that can possibly happen and all these events are equally likely. For events 1, 4 and 5 you can calculate a theoretical probability.
>   - For many events you can list the possible outcomes, e.g. it will rain tomorrow, it will not rain tomorrow, but they are **not** equally likely. If I am in the middle of a desert where it usually rains only a few days in a year the probability of rain tomorrow is **not** $\frac{1}{2}$. If I know that last year it rained on 7 days of the year I could estimate the probability as $\frac{7}{365}$. In another place in the monsoon season rain tomorrow would be almost certain. I need some kind of experimental evidence to estimate the probability of rain.

Activity 2: What's the probability?

- Photocopy of page 156 for each group 3
- Pieces of paper or card numbered 1 to 10 for each group of 3

Groups of 3   *40 minutes*

Thinking about what might happen

Shuffle your set of cards and place them **face down** on the desk in front of you.

Before you turn over the top card decide between you what the answer to this question is:

*What is the probability that the top card in the pile is **even**?*

Discuss this with your group and write down your answer.

Turning over the card

Turn over the top card – was it even? Record your answer.

Do not put the card back in the pack.

Now answer the same question for the remaining cards as you turn them over one at a time without replacing them in the pack.

Think about how you are answering the questions – listen to one another and try to explain your ideas as clearly as possible. When will you know for sure whether or not the card will be even?

Notes

- In this activity the participants are able to argue and debate how many even cards are left in the pack and how many cards there are altogether.

- When the learners try this activity they should use their own language and speak informally. As the discussions proceed it is useful for them to try to use more formal vocabulary, e.g. possible outcomes, number of even cards left, impossible, certain. A worksheet is provided on page 156 to help learners to record in a systematic way. The worksheet includes an additional 3 card activity from Classroom Activity 2 which you may like to try.

- This activity emphasises that theoretical probability tells you what *might* happen on the next trial. Only when you turn over the card can you be sure.

Classroom Activities for Learners

Activity 1: What's the chance of these events?

- String; pegs; paper
- Showboards or large sheets of paper

Groups of 3, whole group   *40 minutes*

Putting events in order of probability

Each group of 3 should write these events on pieces of paper

You will also need the event written large on showboards or A4 paper for class discussion

1. I will throw a dice and get a four

2. Our teacher will set Maths homework today

3. If Manchester United played the school football team our team would win.

4. I will toss a coin and get heads.

5. There are 4 red balls and one blue ball in a bag. Without looking, I take a ball and get a blue ball.

6. It will rain tomorrow.

Ask each group to choose any 3 events and arrange them in order from least likely to most likely. Choose a spokesperson for your group who will explain **why** you have placed the events in that order.

Ask a group to the front to hold up their 3 chosen events (written large on showboards) in order from least to most likely. The spokesperson must explain their reasons.

Making a probability washing-line

Stretch a piece of string across the front of the room or, if you have no string, draw a line on the board. Write *impossible* at one end and *certain* at the other. Impossible (no chance) is represented by 0. Absolutely certain is represented by 1. So a fifty-fifty chance would be in the middle of the line. Ask the group to peg their 3 paper events to the line.

Ask the learners to add in more events until all 6 events are pegged to the line.

> **Notes**
> For some events you can calculate a theoretical probability. For some events you can carry out an experiment or consider existing evidence to help you decide what is likely to happen. But whether you have a theoretical or an experimental probability you cannot know for sure what the next outcome will be.

Activity 2: What's the probability?

- Pieces of paper or card numbered 1 to 10 for each group of 3 learners
- Worksheet on page **156** for each group of 3
- Showboards

Groups of 3   *40 minutes*

Introductory task for whole class with just 3 cards

Show the class 3 large cards numbered 1, 2 and 3. Shuffles the cards and place them face down on the desk in front of you. Ask:

What is the probability that the top card in the pile is odd?

Give time for discussion in pairs. If necessary, prompt the learners to think about how many of the cards are odd. Then ask for answers on showboards.

Now hand the top card to a learner who shows everyone. It might be odd, it might be even. **Do not put the card back in the pack.**

What is the probability that the new top card is even?

Discuss and work out the probabilities. Hand out the recording sheet on page **156** and help the learners to get started first on the 3 card and then the 10 card activity.

Tasks for each group of learners with 10 cards

Shuffle your set of cards and place them **face down** on the desk in front of you. Do not peep to see the cards!!!

Before you turn over the top card decide between you what the answer to this question is:

*What is the probability that the top card in the pile is **even**?*

Turn over the top card – was it even?

DO NOT put it back in the pack.

Now answer the same question for the remaining cards as you turn them over one at a time without replacing them in the pack. Think about how you are answering the questions – listen to one another and try to explain your ideas as clearly as possible. When will you know for sure whether or not the card will be even?

When you have finished ask for a new question, shuffle the cards and start again!

> **Teaching ideas**
> - Solutions to 10-card activity
>   - The probability the first card is even is $\frac{5}{10}$. You can write this as 0.5 or $\frac{1}{2}$.
>   - After this the probability for the next card will be either $\frac{5}{9}$ (if the first card the group drew was not even) or $\frac{4}{9}$ (if the first card they drew was even
>   - Notice that at each stage the denominator is the number of cards left and the numerator is the number of evens left in the set. Once all the evens have been drawn the probabilities will be zero.
> - The activity can be repeated using **new questions**, e.g. What is the chance that the top card in the pile is greater than 3? What is the chance that the next card is a higher number than the card you have just turned over? (See page 155 for a way of turning this last question into a people maths activity.)

Changes in my classroom practice

Implementing the teaching strategy

Discussion	see page 8

The discussion in this chapter is designed to draw out all the ideas about probability that the learners already have. The teacher then needs to introduce more formal language and give the learners lots of opportunities to use and understand the formal language.

The idea of an event is central to developing an understanding of probability – encourage the learners to learn to say things like:

- The **event** we are interested in that the number is odd.
- The outcomes are **equally possible**.
- If we get a 1, 3, 5, 7 or a 9 we have a **success**.

Obviously this is not how the learners will talk initially so you will need to listen to what they saying in their own words and repeat it back to them using more formal language.

As the participants discuss the events they will refine their understanding of the language that is used. This language needs to be very precise and the differences in meaning are often difficult to understand.

Key questions

- What event are you interested in?
- How many cards have you got left?
- How many even cards have you got left?
- Tell me a situation where it is possible to find a theoretical probability.
  e.g. Picking, without looking, a T-shirt from a drawer containing 3 white and 2 red T-shirts.
- Tell me a situation where it is not possible to find a theoretical probability and you would have to gather evidence and make an estimate based on the experimental evidence.
  e.g. Probability that my bus to town will arrive on time.

Follow up activity

Higher or lower

*You will need: a large space inside or out, 10 showboards or 10 large sheets of paper with one of the numbers 1 to 10 written on each, a **sign** saying LARGER and a **sign** saying SMALLER.*

The activity of drawing a card from a set of cards numbered 1 to 10 works well as a people maths activity.

Shuffle the showboards with the numbers from 1 to 10 on them and ask 10 learners to stand at the front holding them so that no one can see their number. Place a sign saying **Higher** on one side of the space and a sign saying **Lower** on the other side.

1. Ask the first learner with a showboard to turn around and show their number. In the game in the picture below the first number was 7. **Will the next number be Higher or Lower?**

   Learners need time to think and make a sensible guess knowing how many higher numbers are still hidden.

   If first number is 7, as in the picture below, then next number is likely to be lower because only numbers 8, 9 and 10 are higher.

Game with 4 numbers revealed

2. Tell the learners that when you say NOW they must move either to the Higher sign or the Lower sign.

3. Tell the learner with the next number to turn round. If the number is higher then everyone who chose lower is **out** and must sit down. If it is lower then it is the learners who chose higher who are out.

People who chose lower

People who chose higher

4. Those who **chose correctly are still in the game.** Now they have to decide whether they think the next number will be higher or lower. The game continues until all the numbers have been revealed. When the first game has finished, shuffle the numbers and play again until the learners are making really good choices about what is likely to happen.

3 card activity

Place cards numbered 1, 2, 3 face down. What is the probability that the top card is odd?

Fill in the probability and discuss your reasons before turning over the card.

Now discuss the next card.

Number of cards in pile	Probability top card is ODD	Our reasons	When we turned over the top card ...
3	$\frac{2}{3}$	There are 2 odd cards 1 and 3	It was number....
2			
1			

10 card activity

Repeat the activity this time using cards numbered 1 to 10 and giving the probability of an **even** card.

Number of cards in pile	Probability top card is EVEN	Our reasons	When we turned over the top card
10			It was number ...
9			
8			

Asking questions

Teaching strategy: Visual and practical learning styles

Curriculum content

Data collection by asking questions relating to social, economic and environmental issues

Prior knowledge needed

How to construct and use tally tables

Intended Learning Outcomes

At the end of this activity teachers and learners will:

- Know there should be a purpose for asking a question
- Understand that the outcomes of questionnaires can affect lives, for example, where a new school or hospital might be needed in future
- Be able to design a good questionnaire
- Appreciate how sampling and bias affect results
- Have experienced working with the data cycle

Fact box

Census: A survey of a complete population. For example, a count of an entire country at regular intervals, often every 10 years.

Population: The complete set of people being studied by a statistical method. For example, everyone eligible to vote in an upcoming election.

Sample: A sub-set of the population which should be representative of everyone in it. For example, people from all age groups, incomes, ethnicities and both sexes.

Bias: When the sample does not represent the population. For example only asking the opinions of voters in the towns and not of those living in the rural areas.

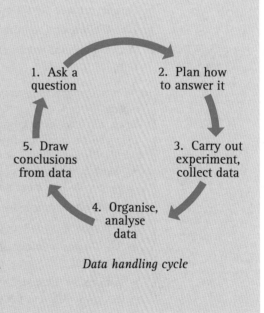

Data handling cycle

Resources for this workshop

Photocopy questionnaire page 162 for each teacher; look for articles on water shortages in local papers or on the Internet.

Workshop Activities for Teachers

Activity 1: A poor questionnaire?

> • Copies of the Healthy Eating Questionnaire below
>
> *Pairs/Group*   *45 minutes*

Healthy Eating Questionnaire

Name: ....   Age: ....

Male/Female: ....   Are you overweight? ....

Sensible people eat fruit and vegetables every day, do you? ....

Which of the following do you eat?
Bananas, apples, oranges, salad, greens, peppers, tomatoes, citrus fruit.

How much water do you drink a day? 0–1, 1–2, 2–3, 3–4,

Answer the questionnaire on your own as best as you can. Then in pairs, discuss the difficulties or problems you had.

Re-write these questions in a more acceptable and sensible way. Add some more of your own. Share the new and re-written questions with the group and try to answer each other's. If there are still some which are unclear or difficult to answer change them again.

In a group, answer the following questions.

1. Which kinds of questions were either easy or difficult to answer, and why was this?

2. Which questions would enable you to collect good quality data on the eating habits of your sample?

Notes

Once you have decided on a topic for a survey you will need a questionnaire that will help you get good quality data that is easy to organise, analyse and interpret.

- Most questionnaires should be anonymous (you do not know who they come from) so people feel more able to give honest answers.
- Don't upset people by making the questions personal or rude.
- Use tick boxes where possible, making sure the categories do not overlap.
- Use a small number of categories and include an 'other' box with room for a comment.
- Make sure the questions are clear and cannot be interpreted or answered in different ways by different people.
- Do not ask questions that encourage or lead people to agree with you (leading questions).
- Once you have your questionnaire try it out on a few people to see if they find it understandable and straightforward to fill in. If not re-write the questions and start the process again.

Activity 2: Sampling and bias

- Articles on water usage or shortages

Individual/Group   *45 minutes*

You are concerned that too much water is being wasted in your area and decide to conduct a survey to gather more information.

Write 5 good questions and discuss them in your group. (Use the notes on Activity 1.)

Look at the data-handling cycle on page **157** noticing the five stages. Check that your questions will provide data that you can organise and analyse.

In your group discuss and write down answers to the following questions:

- How many people will you ask to fill in your questionnaire? (Sample size.)
- Which groups will you ask?
- How will you try to avoid getting a biased sample of people?

> **Notes**
> - Different groups of people in your community will have different and probably conflicting priorities for the use of water. For example, the farmer irrigating his crops, the health worker concerned about poor sanitation or the family wanting good drinking water. If you only ask one of these groups your answers will be biased in favour of that group. In a good sample it must be possible for all groups to be represented, either by random selection or in proportion to the numbers of each group in the total population.
> - Depending on the questions you have written down, you might want to make sure you ask both males and females, as well as people of different ages.
> - Be aware of any issues specific to your community.
> - Collect articles from newspapers or magazines, particularly those with examples of graphs, and display them in your classroom.

Classroom Activities for Learners

How is water used in my community?

These activities provide the opportunity to work through the data cycle, to present a project and to build awareness of social, economic and environmental issues.

Activity 1: How do you access your water?

> • Data-collection sheet (page 162)
>
> *50 minutes*

Where do you get your water?

The possible answers to this question will vary depending on where you and your learners live. Ask your learners for suggestions and write them on the board.

You will need a data collection sheet with the categories and tick-boxes. Don't forget to add one labelled 'other'. (See the data-collection sheet page 162 (Activity 1) for suggestions.)

Will you ask your learners to tick one box only, or is it more appropriate for your area that they have more than one source? Should they just tick the main one?

Activity 2: Apart from food, drink and personal washing, what else do you use water for?

> • Data collection sheet (page 162)   *50 minutes*

As with Activity 1, make this personal to your learners and where they live. Ask them for suggestions and write them on the board.

Decide on the final categories for the data collection sheet, not forgetting one labelled 'other'. (Turn to page 162 (Activity 2) for suggestions.)

This time the learners should tick all the boxes that apply to them.

Notes on Activities 1 and 2

- Individual answers need to be collected and shared to form Class Results. Large classes could form groups and present Group Results instead. (See page 162 for examples of possible tally tables.) How you organise the collection of the individual answers into a tally table of results depends on the number of learners and space in the room.

- Has your community's access to and use of water changed over the last few years? Or across the generations?

- To find out, the learners should give the same questionnaire to an older member of their household and ask them to answer the questions about when they were young. In groups of about 10 or 12 the learners share their results in two separate tally tables, one for their own answers and one for the older generation. They then draw separate or double bar charts and compare the two sets of results. They should write a few sentences explaining what is similar and what is different between the two sets of results, and report back to the class.

Activity 3: How much water do I use?

Example of tally chart page **162**.

What do I use water for?

From Activity 2 you should have a list of things water is used for in your community. To this the learners must now add drinking, preparing food, cooking, washing up, washing themselves, cleaning teeth and anything else they might use water for. Ask for suggestions and decide on your list as a class.

How much water does it take?

For each activity on the list you now need to estimate how many litres of water are used. This can vary widely across countries and communities. For example, how much water it takes to clean your teeth will depend on whether you use a mug of water or keep the tap running. Modern washing machines can use much less than older models.

How often do I do each activity?

Decide on the time scale for collecting data. A 'typical' day or 24 hours or 'over the weekend' will be long enough. Each learner will need a tally chart to collect and record their data. (See example on page **162**.) They can then add up how many litres of water in total they have used in the time period and bring this back to class.

> **Stage 1: Ask a question**

> **Stage 2: Plan how to answer it**

> **Stage 3: Collect data**

Notes

- You could have a lesson on 'Measurement' or 'Volume' in preparation for collecting the data. Ask the learners to fill various containers with water and measure the volume in litres. If they know the actual capacity of some glasses, mugs, bowls, etc. it will help them to estimate the volume of water held in similar containers. Look at brochures and advertisements to find out how much water washing machines, showers or irrigation systems use. If you can access it, try searching for such information on the internet.

- How you collect the data from each learner will depend on your class.

  You might prepare a sheet for them to write on as they enter the class, or a spreadsheet if you have a laptop. If you have a very large class, divide the learners into groups and let each group calculate its own mean and range. They should write the number in the group, the mean, the highest and lowest values on a showboard so you can collect this data to work out the class mean and range.

  > **Stage 4: Organise and analyse data**

- Encourage your learners to write sentences comparing their own or their group's results with some others in the class. How might their results be different from learners in other countries? Can you find this out? (See end of this chapter for some ideas.)

  > **Stage 5: Draw conclusions**

Activity 1

How do you access water?

(Tick one box only)

Tap in house or on premises

Communal tap

Rainwater tank

Borehole

No formal access to water

Other

Add another category if you have one more appropriate for your area

Activity 1

How do you access water?

Group or Class results

	Tally	Frequency
Tap in house		
Communal tap		
Rainwater tank		
Borehole		
No formal access		
Total		

Activity 2

Apart from food, drink and personal washing, what do you use water for?

(Tick all boxes that apply to you)

Flush toilets

Washing machine

Clothes washing by hand

Dish washer machine

Dish washing by hand

To water garden

To water vegetable patch

To irrigate larger piece of land

Add another category if you have one more appropriate for your class

Activity 2

Apart from food, drink and personal washing, what do you use water for?

Group or Class results

	Tally	Frequency
Flush toilet		
Washing machine		
Wash by hand		
Dishes by machine		
Dishes by hand		
Water garden		
Water vegetables		
Irrigate land		
Total		

Activity 3

Make a data collection sheet with the activities you and your learners have listed. The one below has been started. Add your own activities and the time scale of your survey. After the lesson on measurement and volume, you can fill in the number of litres you estimate will be used for each activity

Data Collection Sheet – Water used on ....

Name : ....

Activity	Litres each activity	Number of times	Total litres used
Drinking			
Preparing food			
Cooking			
Washing up			
Washing hands			
Using toilet			

Notes to help you lead the discussion
Many school curricula have as one of their aims the education of the learner in citizenship. The learner should be aware of social, economic and environmental issues as they effect both the local and global situations. By collecting data locally, the learner becomes actively involved in their own learning. If the teacher or learner can provide global comparisons, there is the opportunity for critical analysis and the development of ideas of citizenship.

Resources

Collect articles, reports, graphs or anything relating to statistics from newspapers and magazines.

Encourage your learners to do the same by making a scrapbook or display corner.

When you hear a statistic quoted on the radio, write it down. Is it true? Could your class investigate it?

Use the internet. When you find an interesting site, bookmark it so you can find it again.

http://www.unwater.org/worldwaterday/
http://www.statssa.gov.za/
http://censusatschool.org.uk/

World Water Day – 22 March

The United Nations has declared 22nd March 'World Water Day', with the aim of increasing knowledge and awareness of the importance of water. They produce promotional materials every year that could be used in your classrooms. The statements below are taken from these materials.

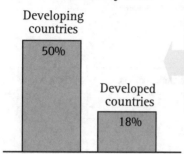

Increase in water withdrawals by 2025

There is expected to be no more water available in 2050 than there was in 2007.

By 2025 water withdrawals are predicted to increase by 50% in developing countries and by 18% in developed countries.

World population is expected to increase from 7 billion in 2012 to 9.3 billion in 2050.

The resulting demand for food will increase by 70% by 2050.

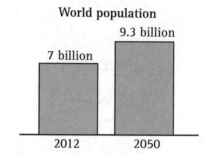

World population

In the last century water use grew at more than the rate of population increase.

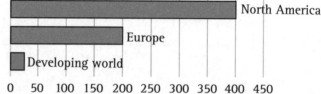

Approximate litres a day for drinking, washing and cooking

The average person in the developing world uses 20 litres of water a day for drinking, washing and cooking. In Europe they would use approximately 200 litres and in North America more than 400 litres a day.

Every day people drink 2-4 litres of water but the food they eat takes 2000-4000 litres of water to produce.

Agriculture accounts for 70% of global water withdrawals, up to 90% in some fast-growing economies.

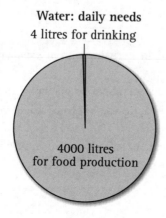

Water: daily needs

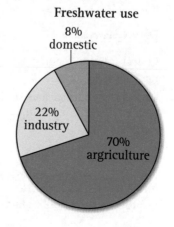

Freshwater use

Representing data graphically

Teaching strategy: People Maths

Curriculum content

Organising, summarising and displaying large data sets

Prior knowledge needed

The difference between discrete and continuous data

Intended Learning Outcomes

At the end of this activity teachers and learners will:

- Know how to construct different graphs to represent data
- Understand when to use the different averages
- Be able to make comparisons between different population groups
- Appreciate how well or not an average represents the data
- Have experienced working with the data cycle

Fact box

Median: The middle value when all the data has been put in numerical order. If there is an even number of pieces of data, calculate the middle (mean) of the middle pair of values.

Mode: The data value that you have most often.

Modal group: The group that contains the greatest number of pieces of data.

Range: The numerical answer when you subtract the smallest from the largest data value.

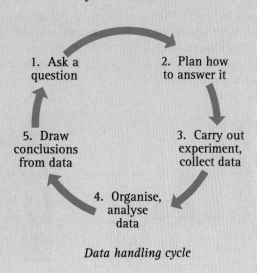

Data handling cycle

Resources for this workshop

Timer or watch showing seconds; post-it notes; counters or bottle tops; marker pens string; pair of compasses.

Workshop Activities for Teachers

Activity 1: Are you good at holding your breath?

- Timer or watch showing seconds; post-it notes
- Board or empty wall space

Pairs, whole group   *40 minutes*

Your group will be much smaller than the classes you teach so the task is different. Work through these activities to make sure you understand the processes, then discuss how the organisation of activities might be different if you used learners instead of pieces of paper or counters (see classroom activities for learners).

Collecting the data

Work with a partner, one of you holds your breath while the other one times how long you can do this for. Write down your time, in seconds on a post-it note (or piece of scrap paper). Have at least two goes each, writing each time on a separate post-it note. **Try this now**

Combining data from everyone in the group

Move to the board and stick your post-it notes in a row from the shortest time to the longest time. Aim to collect at least 20 separate bits of data. Move the first and last post-it notes (i.e. the shortest and the longest time) to a space above your row. Repeat for the second and second to last post-it notes. Continue until you are left with either just one or two post-it notes. If you are left with just one, the time on the paper will be the median time a member of your group can hold their breath. If you have two times left, the median time is exactly in between the two remaining times.

The data you have collected is continuous data. Discuss in your group the difference between continuous and discrete data.

Look at the data and decide on sensible groupings. You should aim for 4 to 6 separate groups, possibly with a range of 10 or 15 seconds, depending on your data. Draw a continuous scale on the blackboard, mark off the groups, then move your post-it notes, one at a time, into the correct group. Take care to stack the notes in a neat grid, lining up with each other both horizontally and vertically.

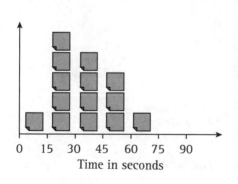

Teachers making a bar graph

What is the modal group for your data? Does the median lie in this group? What does this mean?

Activity 2: Do I come from a big family?

Stage 1: Ask a question

- Counters or bottle tops. Marker pens or sticky dots
- Plain paper, thin string, cotton or wool, pair of compasses

Whole group

Stage 2: Plan how to answer it

30 minutes

To prepare for constructing a pie chart with your class, this alternative task uses counters instead of people. If you know there will only be a small group at the workshop, collect some extra data from other teachers in your school first. 15–20 answers in total is enough.

Ask each teacher the following question: 'How many children did your mother have?'

The teacher takes a counter and writes their answer on it (or on paper stuck to the counter or on paper put inside the up-side-down bottle top). Is this data discrete or continuous?

Stage 3: Collect data

Arrange the counters in a line, in numerical order and write down the median number of children born to one mother (see Teachers' Activity 1). Mark a dot in the middle of a sheet of plain paper. Carefully place the counters, still in order, to form the circumference of a circle centred on this dot. Think about and discuss how you could make this circle of counters as accurate as possible. The counters should touch.

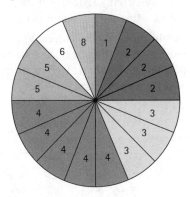
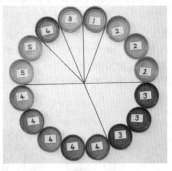

Pie chart with bottle tops

Stage 4: Organise and analyse data

To draw in the sectors of the pie chart, hold one end of a piece of string on the centre dot and the other end at the touching point of the counters labelled 1 and 2. Draw a straight line. Repeat round the circle until all the different sectors have been drawn (see diagram for Classroom Activity 2). Label the sectors, then remove the counters. Use a pair of compasses to draw in the circle.

What is the modal number of children born to the teachers' mothers? Compare the median number with the modal number and answer the question for Activity 2.

Stage 5: Draw conclusions

> **Notes on Activities 1 and 2**
> These activities are to prepare you for working with large numbers of learners in your classrooms. Make sure you are confident with the mathematical concepts and techniques. Discuss with the other teachers at the workshop any problems you think might arise and try to think of possible solutions. Talk about how and where the five stages of the data cycle apply to these two activities.

Classroom Activities for Learners

Activity 1: Am I Average? (Part 1)

- Poster-sized plain paper; thick rope; metre ruler; sticky tape
- Everyone should know their height in cm

Whole class   *30–45 minutes*

Divide your class into two groups, boys and girls, and do the same activities with both. Find a large space, perhaps outside, and tell each group to line up in order of their heights, shortest to tallest. Get someone from each group to do a visual check until you and they are convinced every learner is in the correct place.

Tell the first and last learner (shortest and tallest), to take one step forwards, out of the line. Repeat, the new first and last taking one step forward, as a pair, until there is either one person or two people left. If there is only one person write down their height, it is the median height of the group. If there are two people left, measure both heights and the number exactly in-between will be the median height (see diagram in Teachers' Activity 1).

Change the ordered line into a grouped frequency chart. Mark a line on the ground, a thick rope could be used outdoors, or use the outside wall of the classroom. Decide on which groups to use and put labels on the wall or ground, such as 110 cm, 120 cm, 130 cm, 140 cm, 150 cm, 160 cm, 170 cm. The labels should be placed out in a line with $\frac{1}{2}$ metre gaps.

Starting with the shortest person, the girls move in turn into the correct group, making 'bars' at right angles to the line or wall. Each person must take up the same space in each bar, so check they form a straight line with the person to their left and right as well as in front and behind. The boys do the same to make a second grouped frequency chart.

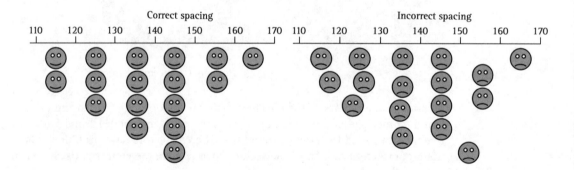

Teaching ideas

- It is not necessary for every learner to know their exact height, just which group they belong to. Measure from the floor, up a wall, and mark the height boundaries, 110 cm, 120 cm, 130 cm, etc. with chalk or sticky tape at different places along the wall. The learners then only need to find and remember which heights they come between. If you choose groups from 110 up to but not including 120 then a learner who is exactly 120 cm should stand between 120 and 130.

- Compare the median heights of the boys and girls and write your conclusions on a large poster. Compare the range of heights. Is it different? Why?

- The group with the most people in it is called the modal group. Compare the modal group heights of the boys and girls and write it on a poster as before. You could also draw a large version of the two grouped frequency tables to display in the classroom.

- How tall might an 'average' girl or 'average' boy be?

Activity 2: Am I Average? (Part 2)

- Large plain paper; pens; long lengths of string
- Everyone should know their shoe size

Whole class   *40 minutes*

Divide your class into two groups, boys and girls. They should form separate pie-charts so you can make comparisons between the two. Tell the girls to get into groups according to their shoe size. Starting with the smallest size they stand next to each other in an arc, until all the girls are standing on the circumference of a large circle. Draw the largest circle you can on your paper, mark its centre and put the paper on the floor in the centre of the girls. You will need long pieces of string, one less than the number of different shoe sizes. One person holds one end of all the strings over the centre of the paper circle, the other ends are held where the different shoe size groups meet. Draw along the strings, on the paper on the floor, to form a representation of your people pie-chart. Label the sectors and give it a title. Do exactly the same with the boys to construct the second pie-chart.

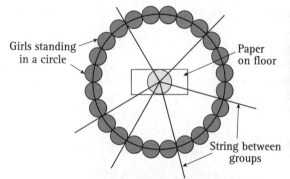

Girls standing in a circle

Paper on floor

String between groups

Teachers making a pie chart

Teaching ideas

- It is useful to get into groups according to shoe size before trying to form a circle. Once the centre is marked and the paper is on the floor, ask the learners about the definition of a circle, or for any facts they know which would help them form as accurate a circle as possible. When the strings are held in place at the boundaries, someone not holding a string can draw the sectors on the paper.

- Use your people pie chart to find the median and modal shoe size for both the girls and the boys. Calculate the range for both and write all your answers on the poster.

- Ask your learners to compare the two groups. Ask which learners think they are 'average'.

Changes in my classroom practice

Implementing the teaching strategy

People maths	*see page 5*

Using your learners in the ways described in this workshop is an effective strategy in very large classes, as everyone gets to participate. If at all possible, take them outside the classroom. If you can find an area where you can draw in chalk on the floor you will be able to draw a large chalk pie chart! Physically moving around, rather than being static at a desk, can help many learners understand the mathematics better. They can be more motivated and engaged with the problem, and recall it more readily at a later date.

The learning becomes much more visible to the teacher and learner. To find the median from a line they can see the importance of moving as a pair. If there is not one middle person but a pair left, they know to find the height exactly in between.

As the group starts to organise itself the teacher can stand back and observe, letting the learners correct each other. Are they evenly spaced in the frequency chart, are they standing in a circle for the pie chart? It is a group responsibility to check and adjust as necessary.

Learners become actively involved with their own learning. Talking to each other and discussing the mathematics is a very powerful way of them deepening their understanding and hopefully remembering and recalling at a later date.

Key questions to develop understanding

This is a way of bringing project work into the classroom. The learners use different techniques of collecting, organising, summarising, analysing and representing data because they have a specific **question** or problem to solve.

Using any of these activities you will have worked through the data handling cycle. Look back and check that you agree. The **questions** can be short and simple or form part of a much bigger project.

The teacher or learner should first ask a question. A plan is then made as to how the answer to the question might be worked out. An experiment is carried out or data is collected in some way. The data must be organised so that it can be processed and analysed. Then it is interpreted and conclusions are drawn.

If the original question has been answered you might stop, but often the data is inconclusive, or only partly gives an answer. In this case you could ask a slightly different question or change the plan, and work through the data cycle again.

Further discussion of activities

Workshop Activity 1: Are you good at holding your breath?

You probably discussed in your workshop that 'good' in this question means 'better than average', but which average and how much better? You only had a small data set so could only compare yourself to a few people. If you have access to the Internet you can research statistics and find out world records for different groups of people. Freedivers, who dive for shell fish without oxygen tanks, can train themselves to hold their breath for a very long time. Is this a helpful skill for any other groups of people?

Many questions ask us to compare two different population groups, such as male to female, young to old, rich to poor, urban to rural, active/sporty to non-active. An initial question might be 'Can young people hold their breath longer than older people?' If you ask this question, how could you collect the data from an older population? Would you restrict the age range of older people? Your learners might think that athletes, or good runners, would have better lung capacity. Letting them help set the questions is an excellent motivator.

Workshop Activity 2: Do I come from a big family?

Another question might be 'Are families today smaller than they were a generation ago?' or 'Are families in Africa bigger than families in Europe?' or 'In India' or ....

You can search for comparison data on the Internet or in books, or ask your learners to collect data from other members of their communities.

Instead of counters or bottle tops, you could use beads threaded on string or wool to form the pie chart. Different coloured or patterned beads would represent the different number of children born to a mother. In the example below 12 teachers were asked about their mothers.

When the beads have been threaded, pull the ends of the string together until the beads form the circumference of a circle, then tie a knot. In the diagram below we can see that four mothers had two children each. The four mothers are a third of the sample of 12, take up a third of the circumference and would be represented by a third of the filled in pie chart. Use pie charts when you wish to show or compare proportions, fractions or percentages.

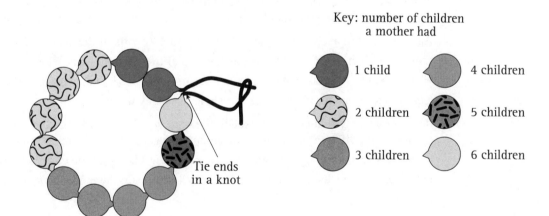

Tie ends in a knot

Key: number of children a mother had

1 child   4 children

2 children   5 children

3 children   6 children

Classroom Activity 1 & 2: Am I average?

Here you are comparing height and shoe size between boys and girls of a similar age. The averages used are median and mode. You could work out the mean, then have a discussion of which average best represents height and which average best represents shoe size? Which of the averages would these people find most useful – health professionals checking babies are growing as they should, clothing manufacturers designing clothes in different sizes, shoe shop owners choosing which sizes to stock? What other information would they also need? Can you think of other people who use averages in their daily life?

The number of children born and shoe size are examples of discrete data: three or four children, size 4 or size 5 shoes. Measuring time and height are examples of continuous data: 25 seconds might have been 24.5 or 25.4 or even 25.4999 seconds before being rounded to the nearest second.

If you draw frequency graphs for discrete data (a bar graph), the bars do not touch, but for continuous data (a histogram), they must touch. When they draw grouped frequency graphs in the classroom, remind your learners of how you decided on the groups and how important it was to know which side of the boundary to stand. In this example, every learner who was at least 110 cm tall but less than 120 cm tall were in one group, someone exactly 120 cm tall would be in the next group. Once they were standing in their group, their exact height did not matter (to group without measuring see notes on Activity 1).

The scale on the x-axis is also written continuously, and not grouped.

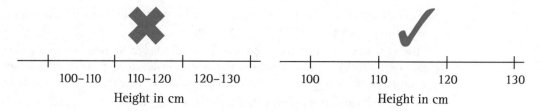

The y-axis is the count of how many in the groups, and is labelled 'frequency'.

Forming pie charts with counters, bottle tops, bead strings or people gives the learners an image of the data making up the complete circumference of the circle. The pie chart must contain all the data. Drawing the sectors between the circumference and the centre of the circle demonstrates the proportional link between amount of data and the angle at the centre.

All the data is represented by the 360°. If there are 32 girls in the class and 8 of them have shoe size 5, then the 8 would make up $\frac{8}{32}$ or $\frac{1}{4}$ of the circumference. The angle at the centre would also be $\frac{1}{4}$ of 360° = 90°. Label this sector Shoe Size 5 and fill in the other sectors as appropriate. Some pie charts mark the angle but many do not.

It is very unlikely that you have exactly the same number of girls and boys, so when you compare their different pie charts you should be aware you are comparing proportions and not actual numbers. You might be able to say something like, '$\frac{1}{4}$ of the girls have shoe size 5 but only $\frac{1}{6}$ of the boys have shoe size 5'. It is easy to compare the mode (biggest sector) using pie charts.

Teaching and learning mathematics with technology

Introduction

The arrival of digital technologies such as computers, mobile phones, tablets (like iPads and Androids) is revolutionising the opportunities for both teachers and learners alike within education in general and within mathematics education in particular. All over the world teachers are looking to develop their personal skills and expertise with technology. 'Technology' includes many things – from computers to mobile devices, from software and applications to websites. There is a lot of technology out there and it keeps changing.

In this chapter we are hoping to point you in the right direction so that you can begin to explore a range of technologies that you can use in your mathematics teaching career and beyond. Technology can support both teachers *and* learners.

For *teachers* of mathematics, technology enables us to create (and display or print) our own teaching resources that include accurate mathematical text and diagrams – and share these with other teachers. We are no longer wholly reliant on buying published textbooks and worksheets – we can create our own and adapt them year-by-year to build our own bank of teaching resources. Technology can also help us to keep a digital record of learners' test scores and help us to analyse learners' progress over time – we can use the information to inform what topics we might need to revisit or when to begin to teach the next topic.

For *learners* of mathematics, technology offers an opportunity for them to be introduced to mathematical ideas and concepts in completely new ways. Mathematical software and applications are available that enable learners to play with mathematical objects in a way that is simply not possible using traditional paper and pencil methods.

In this chapter you will learn about a wide range of technologies that are available to support teaching and learning mathematics.

Fig. 1 Maki Nekhavhambe using a data projector for the first time in her classroom.

Of course, it may not be possible for you to try some of these ideas right away. However as your personal access to technology increases, you can return to this chapter when you are able to try some of the approaches in your own classroom.

Different types of technology

Technology includes a very wide range of devices, software (or applications or 'apps'), websites, etc. that have all been designed for many different purposes and audiences. To help you with some of the terminology, we have included a Glossary at the end of the chapter – so if you come across something that is new to you, look it up!

Also, because there are many different technology products that are available, we cannot provide the specific instructions for all of the ideas we offer – you will need to use the individual 'Help' resources and product manuals that accompany the different technology products – but we hope that you will see the value in making this time investment for yourself.

In addition, there are many online communities and a quick Internet search will often take you to the help you are looking for. The millions of Internet users around the world means that usually someone else has already asked (and published an answer) to the exact question you are asking yourself!

We have organised the chapter by dividing technology into the technologies that might be useful *inside the classroom* with learners and technologies that can be used by you and/or your learners *away from the classroom.*

Technology in the classroom looks at technology for

1. **exploring mathematics** in **a)** number, **b)** algebra, **c)** geometry and **d) statistics and probability;**
2. **projecting mathematics** such as **a)** data projectors, **b)** visualisers and **c)** webcams.

Technology away from the classroom looks at

1. **creating worksheets** by inserting **a)** symbols and equations, **b)** tables, **c)** graphs and **d)** geometric images;
2. **creating resources** to project using **a)** presentation software and **b)** interactive whiteboard software;
3. **creating electronic markbooks** by **a)** entering data and then **b)** making sense of assessment data;

and *technology away from the classroom* looks at

4. **online communities** for teachers and learners hosted by **a)** Ministry of education sites **b)** AimingHigh and **c)** the African Mathematics Initiative;
5. **online resources** such as **a)** Microsoft Maths, **b)** Everything Maths and Science, **c)** Khan Academy, **d)** MathsExcellence and **e)** Math-Aid.

Technology in the classroom

1. Technology for exploring mathematics.

This is technology that has been created to change the way that we engage in mathematics altogether. Such technologies let us get to the 'nuts and bolts' of mathematics and have the potential to engage many more learners in the more challenging mathematical concepts.

a) Number

Spreadsheet software such as a *GeoGebra* spreadsheet or *Microsoft Excel* (which was originally designed for business and accountancy) can be used very creatively to explore number properties. The basic idea is that the columns and rows are labelled with letters and numbers and you use the 'Input' bar to enter text or numbers into the spreadsheet 'cells'. You can then enter data more efficiently by setting up some mathematical rules or relationships! You are not expected to enter each number one by one!

For example, in Fig. 2 below, which shows a 'division table' for numerators and denominators from 1 to 10, only the values in cells A2 and B1 were entered manually. All of the other numbers were made by entering a formula, which was then copied – either across a row or down a column of data. In Fig. 2, you can see that the value of $3 \div 4$ (in cell D5) was calculated using the formula $= \dfrac{\$D\$1}{A5}$. In spreadsheet software the '\$' notation is called absolute referencing – this is important if you want to fix the value of a number in a formula.

	A	B	C	D	E	F	G	H	I	J	K	L
1	divide	1	2	3	4	5	6	7	8	9	10	numerator
2	1	1	2	3	4	5	6	7	8	9	10	
3	2	0.5	1	1.5	2	2.5	3	3.5	4	4.5	5	
4	3	0.33	0.67	1	1.33	1.67	2	2.33	2.67	3	3.33	
5	4	0.25	0.5	0.75	1	1.25	1.5	1.75	2	2.25	2.5	
6	5	0.2	0.4	0.6	0.8	1	1.2	1.4	1.6	1.8	2	
7	6	0.17	0.33	0.5	0.67	0.83	1	1.17	1.33	1.5	1.67	
8	7	0.14	0.29	0.43	0.57	0.71	0.86	1	1.14	1.29	1.43	
9	8	0.13	0.25	0.38	0.5	0.63	0.75	0.88	1	1.13	1.25	
10	9	0.11	0.22	0.33	0.44	0.56	0.67	0.78	0.89	1	1.11	
11	10	0.1	0.2	0.3	0.4	0.5	0.6	0.7	0.8	0.9	1	
12	denomi...											

Number D5: \$D\$1 / A5

Fig. 2 A division table created using a GeoGebra spreadsheet

The power of a spreadsheet is that, by changing just one number in the spreadsheet (the number in cell A2 from a 1 to a 2), a whole new set of decimal numbers can be created. This creates a very motivating space for pupils to explore fraction to decimal conversions and answer questions such as:

- How many times does the decimal number 0.5 appear? Why?
- Can you predict five different fractions that would have a decimal equivalence of 0.33?

b) Algebra

Many of the 'big ideas' and key concepts in mathematics are related to important generalisations, such as that all functions of the type $f(x) = a*x + b$, when plotted on a Cartesian $(x - y)$ graph plane, produce graphs that have a particular geometric feature (a straight line). Most of us will have learned this by rote and believed it because our teachers (and the text book) told us that it was true. However, with technology, it is possible for the learners to observe the graph features for themselves and, by changing the values of a and b, discover much more besides. Within a software packages such as GeoGebra, many linear graphs can be explored very quickly, without the rather slower process of plotting the individual functions by hand using paper and pencil. This does not mean that the learners' graph plotting skills are no longer important – but it does mean that the more important knowledge about the effect that varying the vales of a and b has on the appearance of the linear graphs can be accessed by all learners. Fig. 3 shows an exploratory task in GeoGebra that uses 'sliders' to change the values of a and b.

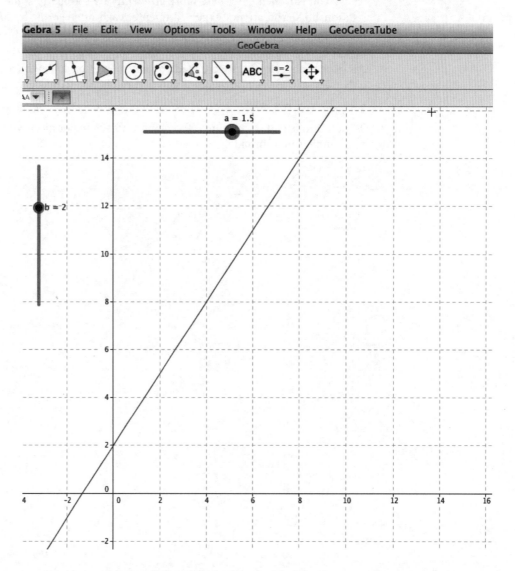

Fig. 3 A GeoGebra file that uses sliders to explore the effect of changing the values on 'a' and 'b' in linear functions given by $f(x) = a*x + b$

It is usually not enough to *only* present this file to the learners and 'show' them what happens. It is better to arouse the learners' curiosity by asking questions such as:

- What do you notice about all graphs for which the value of $b = 0$? (Or 3? Or 5? Or...)
- What do you notice about all graphs for which the value of $a = 3$? (Or 1.5? Or –2? Or...)
- Can you predict what the graph of $y = -1x + 2$ will look like? How do you know?

c) Geometry

Dynamic geometry software has revolutionised the way in which we can understand and explore ideas from geometry. This is because any diagram can be 'interactive' as we can change its appearance by dragging – and explore what happens. We can create mathematically 'robust' 2D shapes that keep their mathematical properties – even when their vertices and side are transformed by dragging. Figs. 4 and 5 show a set of triangles, each of which has been created in the software such that it retains a particular set of properties. Can you spot which triangle is which (and why?).

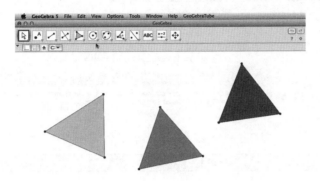

Fig. 4 Three triangles created in GeoGebra

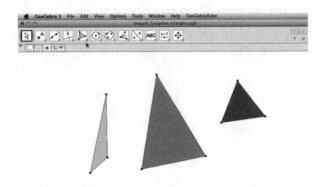

Fig. 5 The three triangles have been transformed by dragging only one of each triangle's vertices!

You really do need to play with constructing these triangles in the software to appreciate how dynamic geometry environments are different – the equilateral and isosceles triangles were creating using a digital set of geometric construction tools. The 'Circle by center and radius' replaces the protractor and mid-points and perpendicular bisectors are built-in digital tools. As with the graphing example, dynamic geometry software does not replace paper and pencil construction techniques. However it does provide a stimulating environment in which to explore geometric constructions and theorems.

Many countries have GeoGebra Institutes that offer face-to-face meetings/courses and online support for teachers (see www.geogebra.org/institutes).

d) Statistics and probability

Any data that has been imported into a mathematical tool such as Excel or GeoGebra can be analysed. A good source of international data on learners' lifestyles and interest is provided by the Census at School website (http://www.censusatschool.org.uk/). The international section of the website shows the many countries that have taken part – and it is possible to request a randomised data set with which to contrast your own learners' data.

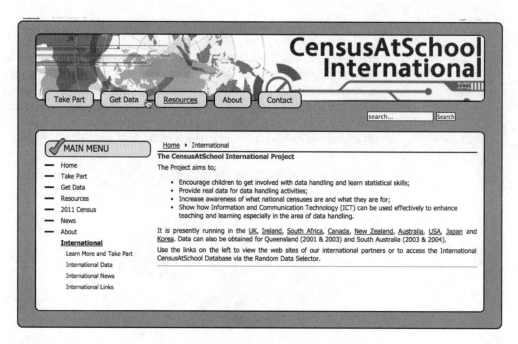

Fig. 6 The international page of the Census at School website

2. Technology for projecting mathematics

This technology is designed to allow you to project images from your tablet or computer to the class. It is not limited to projecting mathematics. You can use it to project any content.

a) Data projectors

A data projector connects to your computer or tablet and projects its display onto a wall or screen. If you had an interactive whiteboard, it would be possible to operate the software on your computer or tablet by touching this projected image and annotate on top using 'electronic writing'.

b) Visualisers

A visualiser is a high resolution camera on a stand that connects to a data projector and, when you place objects, learners' work or a tablet screen underneath it, this image is projected onto the wall display. This is particularly useful when you are doing practical demonstrations as the learners can see your hands!

Fig. 7 A visualiser

c) Web cams

Some computers and most tablets have a built-in webcam, which is a tiny pin-sized camera, usually found on the side of the screen. When the camera is switched on and you are connected to the Internet (i.e. using Skype, FaceTime or similar), this image (usually of your face!) can be seen by others. However, if you point the camera towards some learners' work, you can project this image to a data projector for all in the class to see. It is also possible to buy a low-cost webcam with a bendy arm that plugs into your computer/tablet – and makes it easier to place learners work underneath. This is a low cost visualiser!

Technology away from the classroom

1. Creating worksheets and tests

Creating worksheets and tests with accurate mathematical text and diagrams in word processing software has the distinct (and time-saving) advantage in that you can edit the document again and again to make many different versions.

One of the first IT applications that many people use is a word processing package such as Word to produce typed text that can be saved, edited and printed as and when you need it. This means you can produce your own tasks and tests, write your own helpful notes for your learners and even, by choosing a large clear text (or font), produce posters to display in the classroom.

a) Inserting symbols and equations

The basic letters, numerals and simple symbols such as + and – are all on the keyboard. When you need to use more mathematical symbols such as ÷, × and √ you will usually go to a drop-down menu such as 'Insert' and choose 'Symbols' to get a palette of other common symbols.

$$\begin{array}{cccccc}
\$ & ¢ & £ & ¥ & € & ₠ \\
½ & ⅓ & ⅔ & ¼ & ¾ & ⅕ \\
⅖ & ⅗ & ⅘ & ⅙ & ⅚ & ⅛ \\
⅜ & ⅝ & ⅞ & & & \\
+ & - & × & ÷ & ± & / \\
< & > & ≤ & ≥ & = & ≠ \\
≅ & ≈ & \wedge & \vee & ∞ & \sqrt{\ } \\
\end{array}$$

Fig. 8 A typical palette of more mathematical symbols

To write more complex numerical and algebraic expressions and equations, and to write fractions vertically you will need to use an 'equation editor' which is normally an optional feature of a word processing application. As before, you would select an 'Insert' menu and choose 'Equation', which would reveal a toolbar of different types.

Fig. 9 A toolbar of choices of different types of equations mathematical symbols

b) Inserting tables

There will be many occasions when you want to produce tables and, with your imagination, these can be quite creative!

All of the images in Fig. 10 below have been created as tables within a word processing package – the secret is to learn how to control the size, positioning, text and shading of each cell in the table.

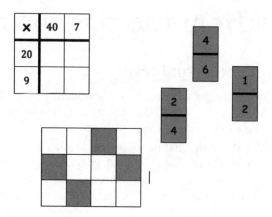

Fig. 10 A selection of different graphics – all created using tables in word processing software

Here are some top tips:

- When you choose to Insert a table, once you have created it with the number of rows and columns that you need, select the 'Table properties' to take control of the size of the rows and columns. Choosing a width and height of 1 cm is very useful for producing accurate images!
- Use border lines creatively – for, example to create the 'fraction cards' above, which can be cut out for learners to match and sort.

c) **Inserting graphs**

Firstly, you must have a Word document open.

In GeoGebra, use the Pointer tool to drag a box around the graph that you want to copy. Open the File menu and choose 'Export graphics view to Clipboard' (See Fig. 11 below.)

(Nothing much will seem to happen.)

Open your Word document and click on Paste.

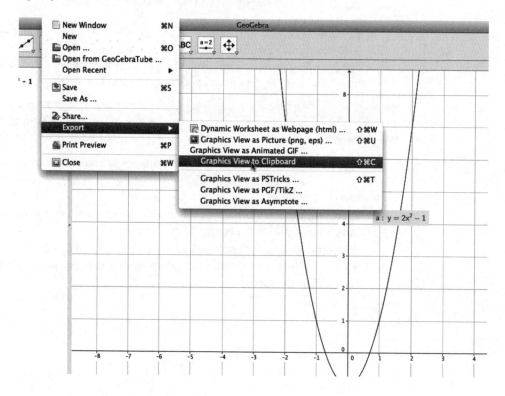

Fig. 11 Exporting a graph from GeoGebra

You can then write the text around your picture.

d) Inserting geometric images

There are a limited range of basic geometric shapes available in most word processing applications when you choose Insert and Shape. However, although you can change the size of them by dragging, you have very little control over the sizes of perimeters, areas and angles. It is much better to create the accurate shape that you want in a mathematical application such as GeoGebra, and then drag around your image to select it and then use the Edit menu to copy it from GeoGebra – and paste into your word processing application, using the same steps for 'Inserting graphs'.

2. Creating resources to project to the class

As soon as you can use a data projector, it is likely that you will want to make presentation 'slides' that can include images from other software (such as graphing and geometry software) to support you to introduce your lesson and provide stimulating and mathematically correct diagrams, symbols and text. You can copy and paste images from other software into such software in the same way as described earlier in this chapter.

a) Presentation software

The most commonly used presentation software is Microsoft PowerPoint but other free software with similar features is available for download from the Internet.

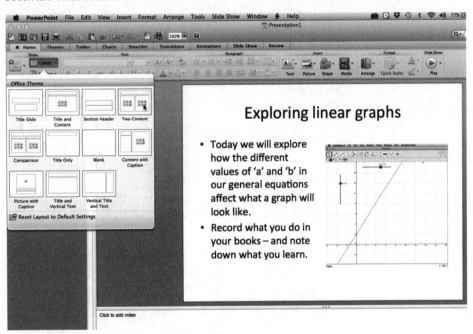

Fig. 12 Creating a slide in PowerPoint

As you Insert each slide into your presentation, you can choose the layout that best suits your lesson. A combination of clear text in a large font size and images (which can be movies) works best.

b) Interactive whiteboard software

If you have access to an interactive whiteboard, which must always be connected to both your computer **and** a data projector, you can use the special software that comes with the board to create presentation files. This software is usually freely downloaded from the manufacturer's website, accompanied by tutorials and help resources to help you make the most of the 'finger touch' functionality.

3. Creating an electronic markbook

Many teachers have found spreadsheet software to be most useful for creating an electronic markbook in which they keep a record of learners' outcomes. The electronic nature of this book means that it is quick and easy to sort any numeric data from highest to lowest values, calculate mean. Mode and median averages and produce graphs and tables to show learners' progress over time. Of course this does rely on high quality assessment data in the first place!

a) **Entering data (Names/dates/marks)**

The starting point is to enter the students' names, gender and the assessment marks.

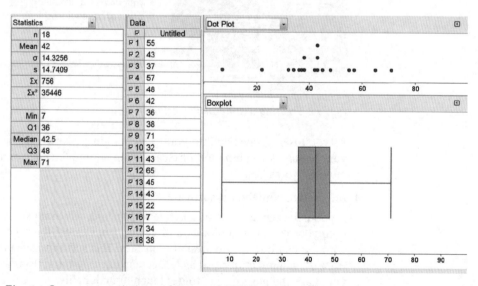

	A	B	C	D	E	F
1	name	gender	Assess1 ...	Assess2 ...	Assess3...	
2	Mensah	F	55	61	62	
3	Ndiaye	M	43	46	44	
4	Nwosu	F	37	41	40	
5	Okafor	F	57	54	53	
6	Okeke	M	48	49	50	
7	Okoro	M	42	41	44	
8	Osei	M	36	38	35	
9	Owusu	F	38	45	39	
10	Sall	M	71	68	70	
11	Sane	M	32	33	35	
12	Sarr	F	43	45	44	
13	Sesay	F	65	66	67	
14	Sow	M	45	47	46	
15	Sy	F	43	46	45	
16	Sylla	M	22	25	31	
17	Toure	M	7	21	15	
18	Traore	M	34	39	38	
19	Turay	F	38	36	37	
20						

Fig. 13 Entering assessment data in a GeoGebra spreadsheet

b) **Making sense of assessment data**

Within GeoGebra, once your data is entered, when you select the column of data you can generate a number of summary statistics and graphs. So for the data on the learners' achievements in Assessment 1, this analysis could be:

Fig. 14 Summary statistics and Box and Whisker plot for Assessment 1

The Box and Whisker plot is a useful graphic that shows the range of marks (71 − 7 = 64), and that 50% of the students were in the mark range from 36 to 48.

If the summary statistics for Assessment 2 are also generated, **as long as** the scales for the *x*-axis are the same, you get a useful graphic that helps you to assess whether the students are making progress over time.

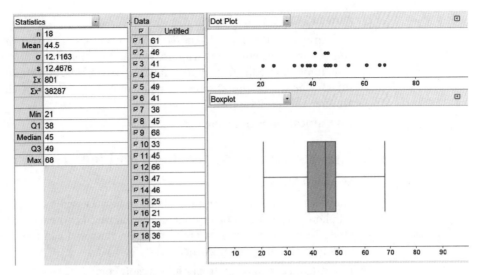

Fig. 15 Summary statistics and Box and Whisker plot for Assessment 2

So it appears that the class is making some progress!!

4. Online communities for teachers and learners

a) Ministry of education sites

Many countries are developing their websites to include information about the curriculum, details of any regional and national testing arrangements and as a gateway or 'portal' for resources to support teaching and learning.

For example:

South Africa: the Thutong website www.thutong.doe.gov.za.

Zimbabwe: the Ministry of Primary and Secondary education website www.mopse.gov.zw.

b) AimingHigh

The AimingHigh teacher network has grown from the hundreds of teachers who have attended the African Institute for Mathematical Sciences School Enrichment Centre's (AIMSSEC) courses in South Africa since 2005.

The website includes Teaching resources, an online Forum and News about the AIMSSEC courses. AIMSSEC work closely with the GeoGebra Institute in South Africa to offer courses and support for technology use.

aiminghigh.aimssec.ac.za

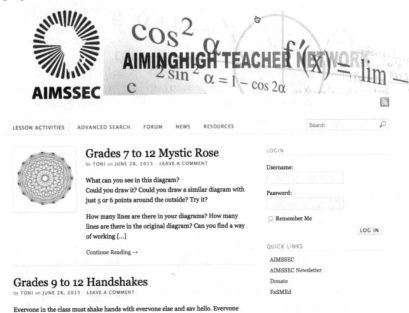

Fig. 16 The AimingHigh Teacher Network homepage

c) African Mathematics Initiative

The African Mathematics Initiative (AMI) is a Kenyan NGO formed by mathematicians and mathematics educators who are working to create a stronger mathematical community and culture of mathematics across Africa. AMI has produced resources to support the use of digital tools for mathematics such as GeoGebra and Scratch, which are available on its website.

www.africanmathsinitiative.net

5. Online resources for teachers and learners

a) Microsoft Math

Microsoft Math is a free resource that can be accessed by high school learners on their cellphones. It includes theory pages and quizzes. Learners can compete against each other. Teachers can create a group for their class and can then keep track of the number of points earned by each learner.

To create an account, go to math.microsoft.com

b) Everything Maths and Science

Everything Maths and Science has free high school textbooks with videos and simulations. The content is specifically created for the South African curriculum but can be used by anybody. The textbooks can be viewed online or downloaded and printed. The site also has a free online practice service that allows teachers to set problems for their learners. Teachers can create a group for their class, set problems and then keep track of the number of points earned by each learner.

www.everythingmaths.co.za

c) Khan Academy

The Khan Academy is an online resource that includes test questions and videos to support learners away from the classroom. You will need to watch the videos carefully too – as they may introduce your learners to a range of different problem solving approaches, mathematical vocabulary and notation. The resources are organised by mathematical topics and they are not aligned to any particular country's curriculum or examination system. If learners create an account, then their progress through the topics is recorded and they are awarded points and rewards for their work.

www.khanacademy.org

d) MathsExcellence

MathsExcellence is a website started by South African teachers to improve the standard of Maths education and to make maths more accessible. It contains many different free resources such as textbooks, videos, tutorials and exam papers.

www.mathsexcellence.co.za

e) Math Aids

Math Aids provides free maths worksheets for teachers and learners. There are many different topics to choose from and because the worksheets are randomly they are all different. The worksheets can be downloaded and printed.

www.math-aids.com

Next steps

Any changes to our teaching practices come at a personal cost. It takes time to learn to use new tools and resources; we often make a personal financial investment in technology that will support us in our work; and in the classroom things might not always go as expected. However, there are very few teachers who disagree with the need to develop personally and professionally as a means to supporting our learners to achieve mathematics to the very best of their abilities.

Glossary

Application or App: These are usually digital tools that have been designed to *only* run on SmartPhones, iPads and Android tablets, although some people are now using this word to describe software. However, many Apps have limited editing and file-saving features. For example, GeoGebra is available as an App, but there is limited functionality when compared to the software version.

Data projector: A data projector projects the image from your computer screen onto a wall or screen so that everyone can see the image. It will usually need a power source and a connection cable from your computer or tablet. The more expensive versions have a more powerful bulb, which means they will project a brighter image.

Dynamic geometry: an interactive mathematics environment that enables geometric constructions to be created and manipulated. For example, 2D shapes can be created and their angles, side lengths, areas and perimeters can be measured. Using the software, these shapes can be transformed by dragging and they retain their underlying mathematical properties, although the measurements may change. The accurate images can be copied and pasted into other software, such as MS Word.

Examples: GeoGebra, Cabri-geometry, The Geometer's Sketchpad, Cinderella

Dynamic graphing: an interactive mathematics environment that enables Cartesian and polar graphs to be plotted automatically by entering the function. The accompanying tables of values can be displayed and the functions can be transformed.

Examples: GeoGebra, Desmos, Autograph

Internet (or World Wide Web): This is a global network that connects everyone's computers to the resources that different individuals and communities have published on their websites.

Mobile messaging application: This is an instant messaging service that can be used on mobile 'phones and computers. It can be a quick way to communicate information in 'real-time'.

Search engine: When you have an internet connection, you use a search engine to look for resources and information on the internet. The most common search engines are Google, Internet Explorer and Yahoo.

Software: A particular digital tool that has been designed for a specific purpose is called 'software'. For example 'word-processing software' allows you to create, edit, save and share files. This text has been written in word processing software.

Spreadsheet: an interactive environment where you can input, organise analyse and store text and numerical data as a table. This data can be displayed graphically and a number of statistical analyses can be used to query and interpret the data.

Examples: Excel, GeoGebra

Web-based: If a particular resource is web-based, you will need to have an Internet connection to be able to access and use the resource. Sometimes you can save the resource onto your own computer so that you can use it 'off-line'.

Formative Assessment

Most teachers include assessment as an important part of their teaching. Traditionally this has been seen as homework and written tests but often marking these assessments can be a chore for the teachers and learners don't always benefit from the feedback – the poor achievers continue to do poorly and this leads to boredom and loss of self-esteem. However, if used formatively, the information obtained from assessments can be used by the teacher to address the needs of their learners and to help learners identify what they need to do to improve their understanding. Throughout this book there have been suggestions of alternative ways to monitor the progress of your learners and to assess their understanding. In this section such methods will be brought together so that alternatives to written tests are made clear.

What is formative assessment?

Black and Wiliam (1998b) suggest that formative assessment can be identified in all activities that teachers and learners undertake where the assessment is analysed to get information that can be used to alter teaching and learning. The assessment becomes formative when the information is used to adapt teaching and learning to better meet student needs. Many teachers react to their learners' responses by giving more time for explanations by the teacher and by the learners themselves. Planning for formative assessment, identifying ways that the learners will make their thinking explicit, by listening to their answers and asking for reasons, will help the lessons become less teacher centred.

The goal of formative assessment is for teachers to monitor students so that on-going feedback can be used to improve their teaching and by students to improve their learning:

- to help learners identify their strengths and weaknesses and target areas that need work
- to help teachers to recognise where learners are struggling and to address problems immediately.

How does formative assessment work in the classroom?

Formative assessment includes teacher observations, classroom discussion and analysis of learner work, including homework and tests. It also includes many informal observations that teachers make as they watch and listen to their learners working on a task. Practical activities, including puzzles and games, can be particularly good for getting learners to talk about their understanding, for getting them listening to others and for appreciating different perspectives.

- Analysing feedback: Marking can be tedious and pointless where the only purpose is to provide a grade for the records. By analysing where the learners have gone wrong or the types of problem they find difficult, a focus can be found for future teaching.
- Classroom observations: Experienced teachers will know the value of daily observations in the classroom to monitor the progress of their learners. Try giving learners opportunities to talk about their work. This can give the teacher valuable insights into their understanding and often reveals aspects that may need re-visiting.
- Purposeful discussion: This can be enhanced with questioning and discussion. Try encouraging the learners to do more talking so that they are encouraged to crystallise their thinking into words

- Learners signals: With a large class, hand signals such as 'thumbs up' for understanding or 'thumbs down' where there are doubts can guide the teacher to the next best steps. Added to some written work, a smiley face, to say 'I am happy with this one', or a sad face to say 'I'm not quite sure' will help the learners' self-assessment as well as providing feedback for the teacher.
- Show boards: Throughout this book the use of individual 'show boards' has been advocated so that the teacher can see the responses of the whole class. You can make simple laminated sheets to enable every individual to show the teacher their response to a question or calculation. In this way you can give immediate feedback and any misunderstanding can be addressed.

Learners' self-assessment

Traditionally, the teacher has been regarded as responsible for the learning of their pupils, but it is also necessary to take account of the role that the learners themselves, and their peers, play. The teacher is responsible for designing and implementing an effective learning environment, and the learner is responsible for the learning within that environment. Particularly within a large class, it is not possible for the teacher to give individuals attention throughout the lesson but children learn in a variety of ways and learning from each other can be effective where the tasks stimulate the exchange of ideas.

Try getting individuals and small groups to keep learning logs, to practise presentations and engage in quizzes. Such strategies involve the learners and their peers in taking responsibility for their learning. The chore of marking written work can also be minimised if first the learners exchange books and the teacher oversees and assists where needed. This can only be achieved satisfactorily if the classroom environment is one of respect and support for those who need it. Pairing high achievers with those who are struggling can have mutual benefit in providing more depth of understanding for both learners. It also acknowledges the fact that in a large class the learners themselves are a valuable resource if they can be utilised effectively by the teacher.

Errors and misconceptions

When teachers know how students are progressing and where they are having trouble, they can use this information to make necessary instructional adjustments, such as re-teaching, trying alternative teaching strategies or offering more models to illustrate a concept. Through experience you will be able to predict where difficulties are likely to occur and make preparation for tackling these, such as using models and images to help understanding, or by allowing time for discussion of new ideas. Planning for teaching must not only take account of the curriculum content but also the learners and their needs that have been identified through formative assessment.

Summary

There are three key processes in learning and teaching:

- establishing where the learners are in their learning;
- establishing where they are going;
- establishing what needs to be done to get them there.

Through formative assessment you can plan to address each of these three processes which will lead to improved learner success and better teacher satisfaction. Every learner is an individual who will respect a teacher who takes account of their needs as they come to recognise their own role in mathematics learning.

http://files.eric.ed.gov/fulltext/ED470206.pdf

Black, Paul, and Dylan Wiliam. "Developing the theory of formative assessment." Educational Assessment, Evaluation and Accountability (formerly: Journal of Personnel Evaluation in Education) 21.1 (2009): 5–31.

Appendix

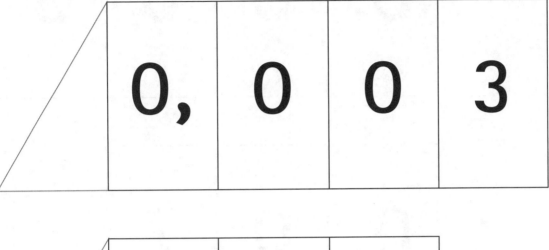

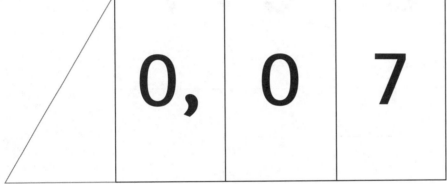

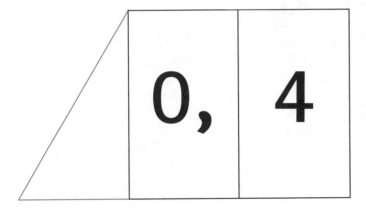

Decimal comma version

Images that help

Arrow cards (or flard cards) give a helpful image of the way numbers are constructed.

Photocopy or make these three cards (arrows cut from cardboard boxes work well).

Place on top of each other to show 0,473 then show how the 7 digit is 0,07 etc.

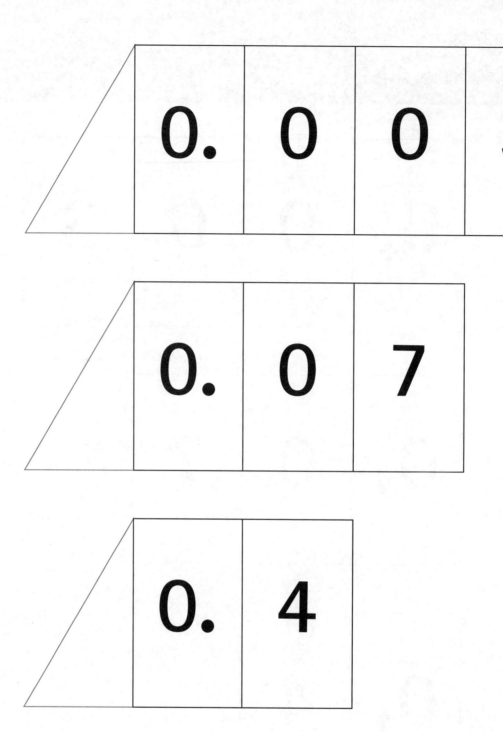

Decimal point version

Images that help

Arrow cards (or flard cards) give a helpful image of the way numbers are constructed.

Photocopy or make these three cards (arrows cut from cardboard boxes work well).

Place on top of each other to show 0.473 then show how the 7 digit is 0.07 etc.

0,6	$\frac{1}{5}$	$\frac{1}{3}$	200%	$\frac{1}{2}$	$\frac{1}{4}$
$\frac{2}{3}$	100%	25%	0,75	$\frac{1}{10}$	30%

of	of	of	of	of	of
is	is	is	is	is	is

36	600	10	200	150	50
100	80	50	1000	300	2000

0,5	$\frac{2}{5}$		3%	5%
0,05	$33\frac{1}{3}\%$		$\frac{1}{3}$	$\frac{3}{4}$
40%	$\frac{3}{100}$		0,75	?

Spinners

Resources needed: card or paper, paper-clip, pencil, scissors

To make a spinner to use instead of a dice photocopy or draw a hexagon.

Pull out one end of the paperclip and pin it to the centre of the spinner with a pen or pencil, then flick the paperclip end with your finger so that it spins rapidly. Check which section of the spinner it ends up on. If you can't decide, just spin again.

Spinners are very versatile you can choose and label a shape to suit your activity

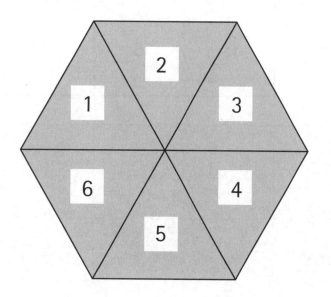

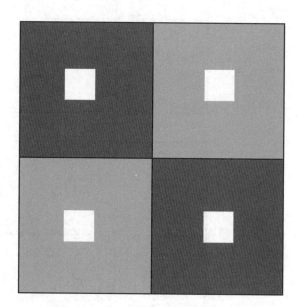

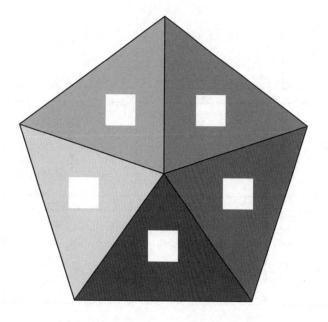

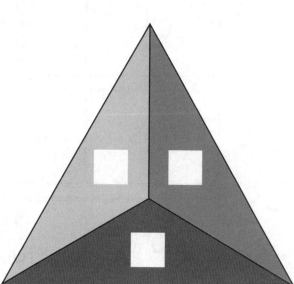

     Appendix: Mathematical Thinking

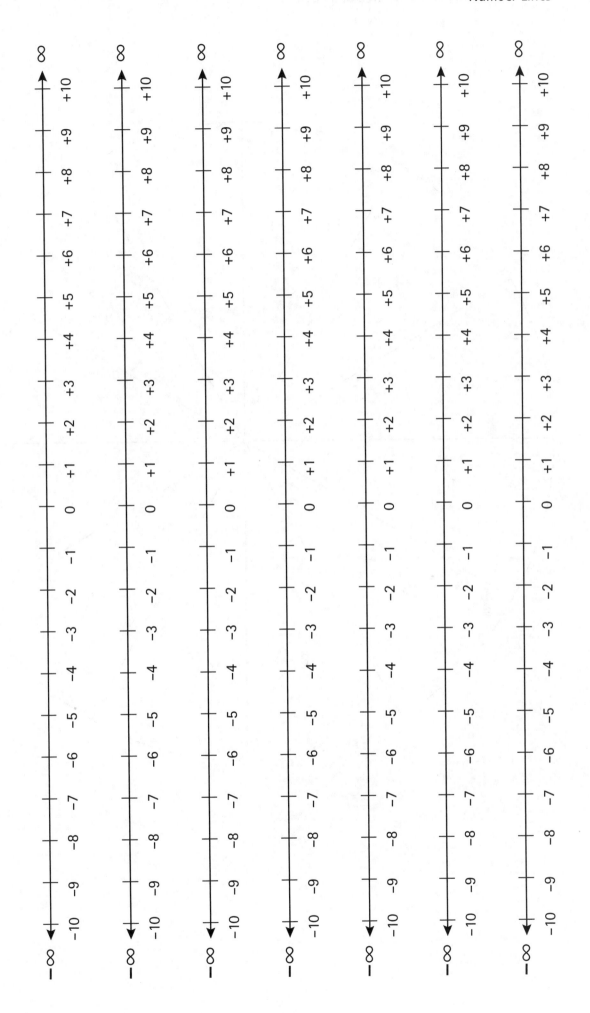

Finding the formula for the area of a circle

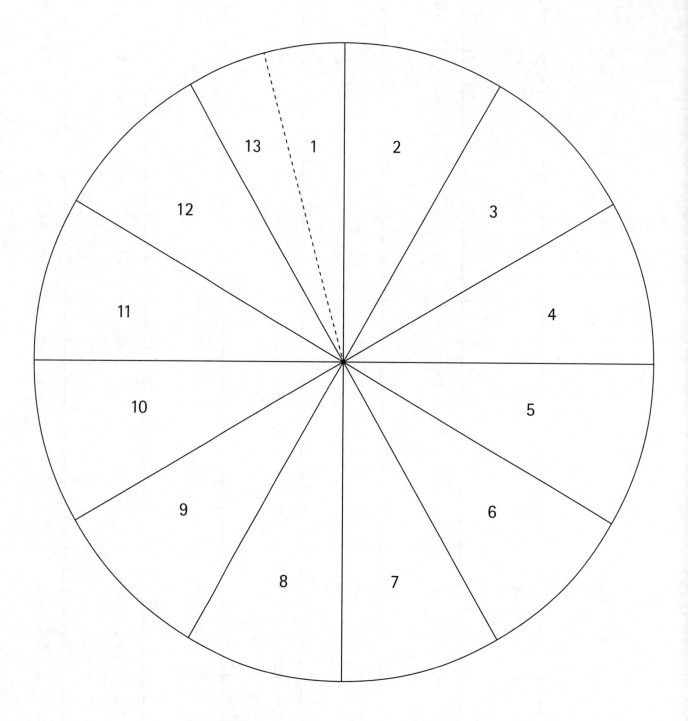

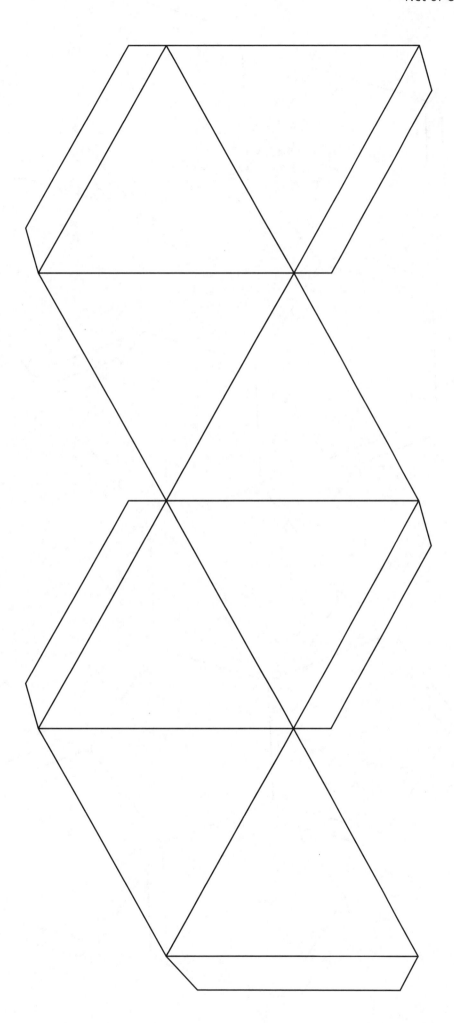

Net of dodecahedron

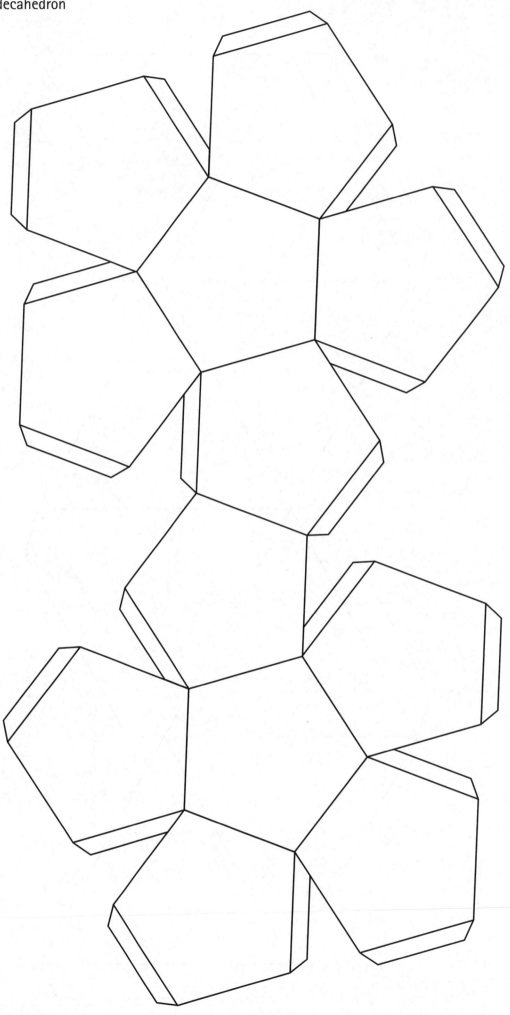

Appendix: Mathematical Thinking

Constructing the net of a dodecahedron in this way gives an interesting exercise in using protractor and compasses accurately and visualizing the ring of 5 pentagons around a central pentagon.

Constructing the net for a dodecahedron

Resources: card or paper, compasses, protractor, glue or sticky tape.

A dodecahedron is made up of 12 regular pentagons

1. Draw a circle of radius 10 cm. Draw one radius faintly. Use a protractor to mark five equally spaced points around the circle. You will need to calculate the angles to measure and use the fact that one whole turn is 360.

2. Join the 5 points to make a regular pentagon. Rub out the radius

3. Draw in the diagonals to make a pentagon star.

4. Now draw in the diagonals of the small pentagon in the centre of the star and extend to touch the large pentagon.

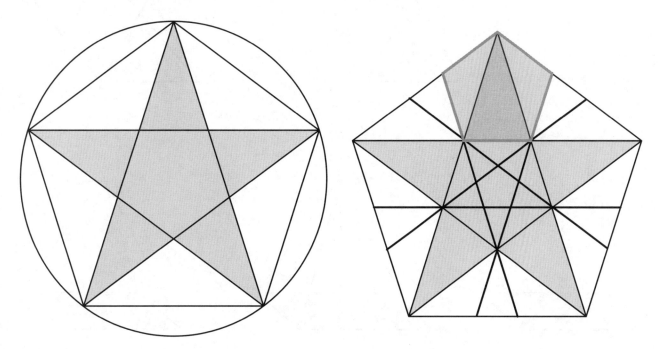

5. **Finding the six small pentagons in your drawing.**

    Each pair of diagonals will create a small pentagon touching the central pentagon.

    The first pentagon is shaded in. Can you find four more pentagons in a ring?

    You now have half the net of a dodecahedron. It is made up of 6 small pentagons. Make another similar net.

    Decide where to put the tabs to join the shape together.

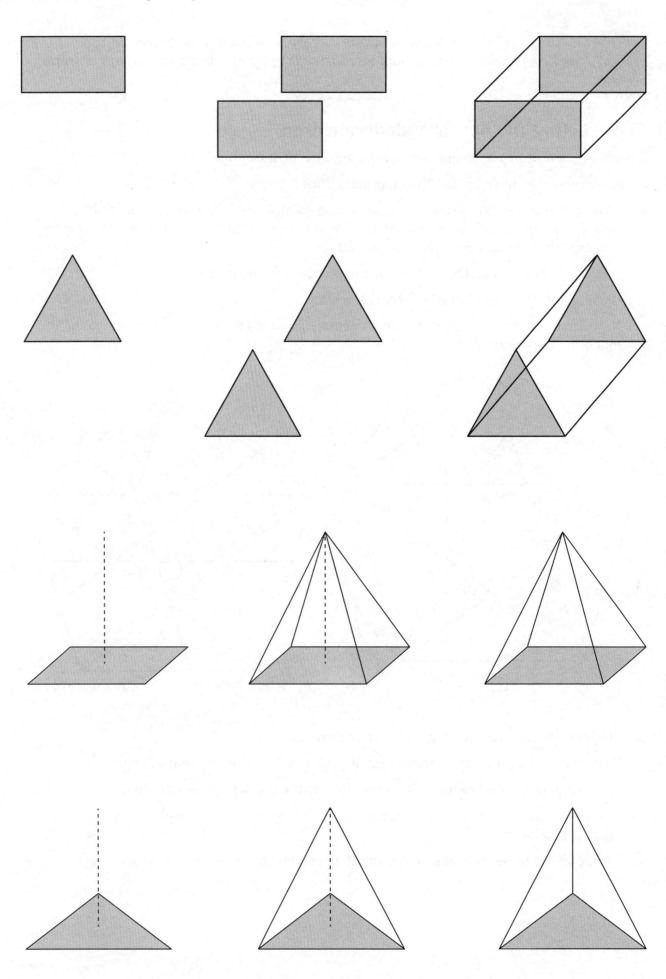

Triangular dotty paper

Acknowledgements by Barrie Barnard, AIMSSEC Academic Manager

AIMSSEC is very proud to acknowledge the work done by the many committed educators to make this publication possible. The seed for the book was planted in 2004 on the very first course which AIMSSEC presented to teachers in South Africa. Toni Beardon initiated the concept design for the book and over the years inspired authors to write chapters and for publishers to commit to publishing the series. The chapters were trialled on several of the twenty-four AIMSSEC courses over the last twelve years. For more information about AIMSSEC please visit http://aimssec.aims.ac.za

For the last two years the project was spearheaded by Christine Hopkins who secured the publishing contract with CUP. Christine collated the twenty-two chapters, while Ingrid Mostert and Julia Anghileri assisted with the editing.

We are grateful to CUP for agreeing to publish the Mathematical Thinking book for the lower secondary age group. We hope that this book will be used in many parts of the world. We salute our volunteers – the editors and authors, the AIMSSEC team, all the tutors and teaching assistants on the courses and of course the teachers themselves, particularly the MT24 teachers who will recognise themselves in the photos in the book.

Editors

Christine Hopkins: Extensive experience of school teaching and teacher training internationally. Former Assistant Dean at Roehampton University. Writing and editing includes professional development material translated into Khmer for the BETT Cambodian Mathematics Project.

Ingrid Mostert: Experience of teaching school mathematics and of training South African mathematics teachers. Currently researcher for the African Institute for Mathematical Sciences Schools Enrichment Centre (AIMSSEC) on the European Union funded project: Formative Assessment in Science and Mathematics Education (FaSMEd).

Julia Anghileri: Senior researcher in the Mathematics Education Team of the University of Cambridge, Faculty of Education. As a writer, editor and internationally recognised researcher Julia has written and contributed to numerous publications in Britain and internationally. http://www.educ.cam.ac.uk/people/staff/anghileri/

Authors

Caroline Ainslie: Founder and CEO of Bubbly Maths, Caroline has written numerous maths shows & workshops, together with accompanying resource packs and presented them in Europe, USA, Africa, Japan and Bali for over 150, 000 children and teachers since 2005. http://www.bubblymaths.co.uk

Toni Beardon: Led and taught on PGCE courses in the University of Cambridge Faculty of Education since 1987 after 25 years school teaching experience. Taught on many professional development courses for teachers. Founded the NRICH family of projects. Founded and directed the AIMSSEC programme of outreach to schools from the African Institute for Mathematical Sciences. http://aimssec.aims.ac.za

Alison Clark-Wilson: Currently a Research Fellow at the London Knowledge Lab, Institute of Education, London working on the Cornerstone Maths project www.cornerstonemaths.co.uk. Designed and led postgraduate courses and projects for practising secondary mathematics teachers at The Mathematics Centre, University of Chichester (2001–2012) Led the EU Comenius funded project EdUmatics, www.edumatics.eu (2009–2012).

Tandi Clausen-May: Since 2009 Tandi has worked as an independent consultant on a range of projects, including national assessments, teacher professional development courses, and mathematics curriculum development at the National Curriculum Development Centre in Uganda. Formerly she was a mathematics teacher, then Principal Research Officer at the National Foundation for Educational Research.

Cynthia Fries: Works on the AIMSSEC programme in South Africa since January 2015, lecturing on both the Mathematical Thinking and Advanced Certificate in Education (ACE) courses. She has written distance learning materials and taken part in interactive broadcasts. Previously a secondary school mathematics teacher for 20 years in Cambridgeshire.

Jennie Golding: Researcher and teacher development at Institute of Education, University of London, following a career to Deputy Head level teaching learners aged 3–93 in schools and universities in England, Australia and elsewhere. Has developed a wide range of mathematics professional development materials and courses, and works extensively in mathematics education policy.

Margaret Jones: Retired Mathematics Consultant. I have had extensive experience of writing with groups, individually and chapters for compilations. Currently editing Mathematic Teaching for the Association of Teachers of Mathematics.

Sinobia Kenny: Local lecturer at AIMSSEC. Responsible for Work Integrated Learning (WIL) in upper primary and lower secondary schools. Worked alongside the teachers who trialled the chapters as workshop assignments therefore has good insight into the needs of teachers in rural disadvantaged schools.

Lynne McClure: Lucky enough to teach on the very first AIMSSEC course!
Taught in schools and universities in various countries, directed the NRICH project and now Director of Cambridge Maths (www.cambridgemaths.org).

Judy Paterson: Died in 2015 and is much missed by everyone who knew her. Judy taught mathematics at schools and bridging colleges in South Africa before moving to New Zealand to teach in high school and then to lecture in Mathematics Education at Auckland University. Her research focused on content-based professional development of teachers and lecturers.

John Suffolk: Helped maths teachers develop since 1974, teaching in universities and working on aid projects in seven countries in southern Africa, Asia and the Pacific. Extensive involvement in assessment, curriculum and materials development and research into learners understanding of school maths.

Diana Townsend: Taught mathematics at secondary school in the UK and to advanced European Baccalaureate level in Brussels, Belgium. Involved in teacher-training of mathematics in UK, S. Africa and Zambia, being part of the AIMSSEC Team on several occasions.

Jan Winter: was a secondary mathematics teacher in Bristol schools before joining the University of Bristol as an education lecturer. Taught on PGCE, masters and other courses as well as on INSET in countries including Sri Lanka, the Gambia and Grenada. Contributed to books for teachers, most recently 'Teaching Secondary Mathematics as if the Planet Matters'.

Photographers: Cynthia Fries and Nadia Baker

Nadia Baker: Teacher of Mathematics at King's Ely Senior School. Previously worked for the Millennium Mathematics Project, University of Cambridge as Schools Outreach Officer. Has extensive experience with the Questacon Science Circus in Australia. She has also taught in Malawi and Nepal, and has experience working on the AIMSSEC programme since 2013.